TWO YEARS IN GOD'S MORMON ARMY

ROSS H. PALFREYMAN

Publishing Services provided by Paper Raven Books LLC
Printed in the United States of America
First Printing, 2025

ISBN 979-8-9874094-9-7 (paperback)
ISBN 979-8-9874094-8-0 (hard cover)

This work is dedicated to my father and my mother. Their unwavering dedication to their beliefs, not only in the doctrine of the Mormon Church, but also in the culture of the Church, directed me toward my mission in God's Mormon Army, and, more importantly, provided me with the wherewithal to develop and pursue an ethical and moral code for my own life.

INTRODUCTION

All experience creates distinctive learning opportunities, and each one of us travels our own unique path through life based on those experiences and how we respond to them. When tough times come, consciously or unconsciously, we fall back on the lessons we have learned from our past to give us guidance in responding to difficulties and challenges. Experience, then, helps to shape who we are.

For two years, I served as a Mormon missionary in the Thailand Bangkok Mission. It was filled with a wealth of experiences that have stayed with me ever since. A couple of years ago, I was reflecting upon just who I was and in what direction I wanted to steer my life. As a part of that examination, I began to read my missionary journal. It immediately became clear to me that being a Mormon missionary has significantly impacted how I have responded to various bumps in the road as I have traveled through life.

Originally, I began this project envisioning only my family as the reading audience. After all, they knew me and so, of course, would be interested. In the alternative, if they were not interested, I could exercise some unrighteous dominion as their father and just order them to read it...and like it. That all changed when a wonderful Catholic friend was visiting our home and spied the first draft of this book on our dining room table. She insisted on reading it and then ingratiated herself to me forever by saying that she loved it. She went on to say that it needed to be published so that other people could know more about Mormonism without actually admitting any interest. She found the transcript entertaining, and at the same time, she learned a great deal about Mormon belief systems. (It is noteworthy that she is still a very happy Catholic.)

While the specific events of my mission are unique to me, the overall course of events cannot conceivably be much different from that of the thousands and thousands of other missionaries who have served throughout the world. I do not pretend to speak for all missionaries, nor do I speak for the Mormon Church. Rather, my account is meant to convey the flavor of a Mormon mission and my reactions to the many events and circumstances I came across. While other missionaries can well tell their own stories, this book is meant to give some insight into what all Mormon missionaries really do.

This account then is written for the thousands of people who have questions about Mormon missions: people who have neighbors whose children go on missions, relatives who have joined the Mormon Church and then sent their children on missions, or those whose bosses or co workers have served missions themselves or have sent their children on missions.

As I have shared preliminary copies of this book with friends, I have found, somewhat to my surprise, that two other groups find this work especially appealing: those who are now being called to serve and those who have returned from their own missions. For those on their way, this is a glimpse of what is in store. Those who once served often find that memories of their own unique missionary experiences come flooding back to them. Ultimately, my goal in writing this book, in addition to attempting to better understand myself... is to share the missionary experience with all those who have wondered just what goes on in "God's Mormon Army."

I

THE CALL

watched the lubricating oil slowly trickle down the pale green wall as my index drill first drilled, then threaded, and finally countersunk aluminum protractor part after aluminum protractor part. After three months of this monotonous manual labor at Vemco Manufacturing, I was more than anxious to get out of the factory and into the mission field. I had volunteered to be a missionary for the Church of Jesus Christ of Latter-day Saints (the Mormons) some three months earlier and was still waiting for my assignment. Usually, once the paperwork was turned into church headquarters in Salt Lake City, Utah, it was only a matter of a month or so before a calling to a specific area of service was received.

In submitting my papers to volunteer to serve as a missionary, I had asked to spend my two years in Tonga. I figured that if I was going to spend two years as a missionary, I might as well do it in an exotic place. My Mormon friends, who also volunteered to give up two years of their lives for missionary service, felt almost unanimously the same way. Not too many of us wanted to stay home in the United States.

One friend in my congregation was promised in a **patriarchal blessing**[1] that he would serve a "foreign" mission. When he received his missionary calling from Salt Lake City, he was notified that he would be serving in the California Oakland Mission. Checking the map, it was apparent to Jerry Smythe, who lived in South Pasadena, California, that the California Oakland Mission could not be classified as a foreign mission. I thought it was all dependent upon how you looked at it; there were parts of Oakland that seemed pretty foreign to me. Nonetheless, he was so concerned over the issue that he wrote to the church leaders in Salt Lake City expressing a willingness to go wherever they assigned him, but reminded them that he had been given a patriarchal blessing stating that he would serve a foreign mission. The power of a patriarchal blessing is rather significant in the eyes of the church, and therefore the church leaders acknowledged the inconsistency by changing his calling from the California Oakland Mission to the Canada Alberta Mission. Jerry Smythe was elated, but I wondered just how "foreign" the Canada Alberta Mission really was.

One good thing about having to wait so long for my mission call was that I was able to save a little bit of money to help my parents pay for the missionary expenses that would be incurred. Missionary expenses are primarily the responsibility of the missionary and his family. As it turned out, I did not stay at Vemco Manufacturing long enough to make too big of a dent in my parents' financial obligations for the missionary tour of duty. In fact, my savings were pretty well exhausted by the time I finished outfitting myself with a new suit, new Mormon underwear, and other missionary essentials.

I remember very distinctly one warm afternoon when I was at my customary duty of drilling out and countersinking very tightly specified holes in the drafting instruments. The lubricating oil was splattering all over my hands, arms, and the navy-blue smock which seemed hardly adequate to keep me clean. My mind had entered the zone wherein it tries to push the body to exceed the work quota established for minimum production purposes. The challenge of exceeding the production quotas was the only way to stay sane in this otherwise extremely boring endeavor.

While I was so focused on my machine and the parts I was running, I could hear the piercing sound of what resembled my mother's voice. I turned to observe that it was indeed my mother, and she was running through the shop towards me waving a white envelope. It was clear that my missionary calling had arrived. I began the process of shutting down my machine and cleaning up so that I could open the long-awaited envelope with its letter from the President of the Church, without ruining it. Unfortunately, I simply was not moving fast enough for my mother, who I think was more anxious than I was to know where her little baby would be spending the next two years of his life. She threatened, "If you don't hurry up, I'll open it!"

It was very rare that I ever saw my mother get overly excited about anything. She had had seven children in ten years, so she was required to take things in stride. However, on this day, the excitement had pretty much overwhelmed her. The only other time I had seen her this animated was some twelve or thirteen years earlier when I had awakened her from a nap by dangling a lizard by the tail over her face. That had turned out to be a bad idea. I spent the rest of the day locked outside, waiting for my father to get home. History with my mother taught me that the frantic look in her eyes meant she wanted the envelope opened now.

I finally got most of the oil cleaned off my hands and arms so that I could open the envelope and read the letter without smudging every thing. I excitedly read that I had been called to serve in the Southeast Asia Mission, specifically the country of Thailand. Mother did not even know where Thailand was and, when I explained to her that it was in Southeast Asia near Laos, Cambodia, and Vietnam, she almost passed out. After all, this was June 1973, and the Vietnam War was still in full swing. Her first words were, "The hell you are! I'm calling Salt Lake." I assured her that I could think of no better place for me to spend the next two years.

I had spent most of my adolescence listening to Walter Cronkite on CBS News provide me with tales of the Vietnam War: head counts, battles and sieges, worthless peace talks, congressional leaders without ethics or morals, and a president telling me how important it was that we stem the tide of communism in Vietnam. I remember listening with fascination to the stories of a recently returned G.I. who had been assigned to be dropped behind enemy lines in Vietnam and fight his way back to the American zone. He told stories of danger and heroism, of death and of the strength of the human spirit. I was fascinated, but I could not help but wonder what the point was of sacrificing so many lives. Regardless, it was to that part of the world that I was headed.

While I did not get to serve as a missionary in Tonga, I could not have been happier with my assignment. The church apparently sensed the need for me to experience some adventure. Some have since suggested that maybe the church just wanted to get me as far away from church headquarters as possible. Whatever the reason for my assignment to Thailand, it did not matter. I was about to embark on a two-year mission for Jesus Christ in Thailand. With just one year of college completed at Southern Utah State College (now Southern Utah University, located in Cedar City, Utah) and no idea of who I really was, I was being asked to tell the Thai people that I knew the way and the truth, and had the light. Somehow that did not invoke fear and trembling in my being, though I suppose it should have.

A Mormon mission is in some ways liberating. In many ways, though, it is like signing up for two years of indentured servitude. In 1973, there were some 17,000 missionaries, virtually all of whom were nineteen years old and full of the exuberance of youth. (I do not mean to ignore a small number of female missionaries and senior members serving missions of a duration shorter than two years who were also numbered among the 17,000 missionaries at the time.) I suppose that due to the logistics of it all, independence of thought and action would create a nightmare for the missionaries' adult leader, called a mission president. Therefore, obedience to rules is extolled as godlike, while creativity and imagination (outside the parameters of the rules) is discouraged as being disruptive and out of harmony with the goals that have been established by **the Brethren**[2] in Salt Lake City. (The Brethren are also referred to as the General Authorities.)

I experienced the authoritarian nature of a mission, and my subservient status therein, almost immediately upon arriving in Salt Lake City, Utah, where I reported to the mission home for one week's worth of preliminary orientation. The mission home was where all missionaries spend their initial week of service. This was definitely a period of orientation and indoctrination. Mormon missionaries came out of the mission home appearing to have all been cut out of the same cloth. White shirts, a tie, dark slacks, clean-shaven faces, and short hair all helped to mark the young Mormon male in his calling. While that was universally the case, it did not mean that each young man had always looked and acted that way before the mission experience.

In fact, my hair was somewhat long and straggly in my pre-mission days, and I knew that it would have to go. For some reason, I had not taken care of the required haircut prior to flying to Salt Lake City. I just figured that I would take care of the matter after dropping my bags off at the mission home. Upon arriving there, I advised the gentleman at the front door that was indeed my intent. He smiled and invited me in, but then would not release me to go back out to the barber, saying I could take care of that later. Well, I had reported some two hours early, and I could not figure out why I had to stay inside the mission home. At the time it seemed of little consequence, and I complied with the instruction. Besides, inside the front door of the mission home was a table full of missionary aids for sale, including journals, notebooks, and pencils. As a young missionary with little in the way of outside knowledge of the situation, I figured I needed one of each trinket offered. After all, it was for sale to the missionaries in the mission home. Looking back, I wish that I had that concession. I wonder who did.

Some two to two-and-a-half hours later, I was sitting in a room full of missionaries, all of whom were just beginning their two-year stints. A middle-aged gentleman stood before us in his dark suit, white shirt, and tie. But my initial impression of him as a gentleman quickly changed to one of a drill sergeant with a hint of jerk. We were told the mission was not a place to have a good time, but that it was serious work, the most important work we would ever do.

In the middle of his speech, his eyes fixed upon my shaggy head. I was then asked to stand for all to see. I guess he needed an example of what a bad missionary was and, having never met me before, he proceeded to tell all present that my long hair was a prime indicator of my ill-prepared spirit. He continued by all but condemning my mission to ruin before it even started. I was somewhat embarrassed by the tongue lashing and a bit put out by it, particularly when I had unsuccessfully tried to get my haircut earlier. I shortly concluded that those who believed what he said were not worth worrying about, and that the rest were already stinging from his overall criticism about our lack of being prepared. I was then invited to sit down.

As I recall, the "welcome" did not last for more than thirty minutes or so, and immediately after my favorite mission leader's departure from the podium, I heard, "Hey, Lebsock!" from the back of the room. As I turned around, I beheld a most welcome sight. Grant Ross and his familiar huge grin had also signed up for the two-year missionary experience. I had previously met Grant Ross in Cedar City, Utah at Southern Utah State College, where he and I played freshman basketball together. The nickname "Lebsock" had come from a road game we played where all of our names had been placed up on the scoreboard next to our jersey number. I guess they thought that "Palfreyman" was too hard to spell, because next to my number "10" was the name "Lebsock." It stuck. Grant Ross and I had about the same skinny build, though he was an additional inch or two taller. (I always resented the fact that my six-foot-one frame never got to my lifelong goal of six-foot-three.) Grant and I laughed about my hair and the perfect example of a bad missionary I had made within the first ten minutes of my mission. He then informed me he was headed to the Taiwan Taipei Mission and that he would be joining me for two months at the **Language Training Mission**[3]

7

in Laie, Hawaii (affectionately referred to as "the LTM"). Neither one of us was quite sure at the time whether that meant we would see much of each other or not, but I took comfort in knowing we would be living this experience in reasonably close proximity.

Meeting Grant Ross at the mission home meant two missionaries that I knew besides myself were going to experience the indoctrination process at the same time I was. Ron Van Dusen was from Arcadia, California, and was headed to the Argentina Buenos Aires Mission. He and I flew up to Salt Lake City together. I always considered Ron Van Dusen a good friend, but I must admit that his sister Debbie was a bigger attraction. She had been my first love, and I still remember her quite fondly.

In a nutshell, the few days spent at the mission home were comprised of a constant bombardment of instruction from health considerations to auto safety, from spiritual preparedness to testimony bearing. We spent time in the temple going through two **endowment**[4] sessions, one of which I recall occurring at 4:00 in the morning. I don't recall very much about it, except that I was not the only one who slept through a significant portion of each of the two sessions we attended that morning.

I had only been through the temple one time prior to embarking on my mission. On that occasion, I was absolutely bombarded with new information and calls to commit myself to things I had not fully thought through. It was not that there was anything untoward, impure, immoral, or unchristian; it was just quite different from the church I knew outside the temple. Outside the temple, my understanding of the gospel was that it was rather simple and straightforward. Jesus Christ taught we should love God and love our neighbors. He was critical of the Sadducees and Pharisees for their adherence to ritualistic rules and rites, to the exclusion of a full consideration of the doctrine of love. Outside the temple, "simplicity" was what I found beautiful about the Mormon Church.

Inside the temple, I concluded that the Mormon Church was almost as ritualistic as the Catholic Church and that, while the admonition not to disclose what went on in the temple was given to protect the sacred nature of the ceremonies, its practical impact was to create what appeared to be a secret society. Personally, I did not see that there was anything all that outrageous that needed to be kept from public scrutiny. In fact, there is a peaceful serenity to the process that always seems present. Regardless, church members are quite circumspect about discussing the temple ceremony, even amongst themselves.

After attending the temple on one occasion, we were all gathered together for a series of lectures. The first lecture was on personal hygiene and health. It was comprehensive, but did not seem to present anything new. Hopefully, the other missionaries in the group also considered the information conveyed as common knowledge. The next speaker was quite humorous in discussing with us the need for all young missionaries to be mindful of automobile safety. If you can imagine speaking to a few hundred nineteen-year-old boys about driving within the speed limit at all times, wearing your safety belts, and making sure to use your turn signals, it would seem to be a topic that could be considered boring for some. This **brother**[5], as we called him, did a great job of conveying the information in a humorous way so as to keep our attention.

Unfortunately for our entertaining brother who reviewed auto safety tips with us, **Elder**[6] S. Dilworth Young spoke next and did not appreciate the humor the way the young missionaries, also called elders, did. The first segment of Elder Young's talk was dedicated to verbally attacking the prior speaker whom he branded as being "light-minded," a breach of his temple commitment, and ignorant as to the importance of the missions that the group of elders were about to embark on.

I felt sorry for that brother. Elder Young was a General Authority and, therefore, in the Mormon Church, he was probably not going to be answerable for his rude and inappropriate comments.

The verbal attack by Elder Young on his predecessor distracted me from much of the rest of Elder Young's message. But I do recall that the gist of his message was that as missionaries we were the literal representatives of Jesus Christ being sent out to the world to spread His gospel, and that the world and each individual therein needed to repent and be baptized into the Latter-day-Saint church. This, indeed, was serious stuff, but throughout the talk, I could not help but wonder if Elder Young was always so strident or if he was just having a bad day.

In contrast to Elder Young, we were provided with an address from one of the Twelve Apostles, Elder LeGrand Richards. Elder Richards seemed old enough to have been around in the days of Joseph Smith himself. Elder Richards was a short, stout man who was as excited about his job as anyone could be. I had heard Elder Richards speak on many occasions in General Conference, a twice-a-year meeting in Salt Lake City where all church members listen to various addresses from church leaders. Rather than fill us with warnings of damnation if we did not behave or doctrinal nuances that would be of little value in Thailand, Elder LeGrand Richards spoke in wonderfully simple terms of his own life's missionary work. He had embraced the light and it had embraced him. I could feel his joy in doing God's work, and I wanted those same feelings for me.

Throughout my five-day stay at the mission home in Salt Lake City, I could not help but continually feel guilty about not being adequately prepared to be the perfect missionary tool in the hand of the Lord. In discussing my feelings with my missionary cohorts, traditionally called companions, I realized that my feelings of inadequacy were shared by many of the missionaries, and that this sense of guilt seemed to act as a catalyst for making sure that we followed the words of our leaders who were clearly more worthy than we were. There were many who felt even more guilty than I did. There always seemed to be a long line of missionaries waiting to confess their sins to the president of the mission home.

Though the mission home experience seemed to drag on unmercifully, it did last only five days, and we were ultimately able to move on toward our assigned fields of labor. On the day of departure, I watched missionaries leave, knowing that their ultimate destinations covered virtually every continent of the globe. This notion that Mormon boys go out to all the world as missionaries to preach the "gospel of Jesus Christ" is a tremendous source of pride to Mormons and creates a true unity of purpose.

My intermediate destination was Hawaii. Murdock Travel made all the travel arrangements, and they were quite creative with my travel arrangements to Hawaii, as well as those of the eleven other missionaries that were traveling with me. Our flight departed from Salt Lake City, went to Boise, Idaho, then stopped over in Portland, Oregon, and Seattle, Washington, before finally pointing itself in the direction of Hawaii. It seemed like there must have been a more direct route, but for a group of twelve nineteen-year-old missionaries it was hardly an inconvenience, especially when in Seattle we were told that the airline had overbooked the economy class seats and therefore they invited us to fly first class from Seattle to Hawaii. We all sensed that this was the way things would play out for our entire missions. After all, we were a part of God's elite Mormon Army.

II

IMMERSION

As we approached Hawaii, I was truly mesmerized by the sight of Oahu and was convinced that my two-year missionary stint would truly be an adventure. Disembarking the plane at Honolulu's International Airport, I spied the traditional Hawaiian welcome with beautiful girls in grass skirts and bikini tops presenting arriving guests with leis around the neck and a kiss on the cheek. It somehow didn't immediately cross my mind that Hawaiians were generally not blondes and that several of the lei-presenting flower girls were. Further, I sadly observed that none of those beautiful girls came over to welcome me, or any of the other eleven missionaries in my group, with a lei or a kiss. Quite frankly, at the time, I could have sacrificed the lei as part of the welcome. I later learned that these special welcomes were reserved for people who had come to the island to spend money. At the time, that was something I clearly did not have. Somehow, I think they knew that. Surviving the disappointment of not getting closer to these wonderful looking greeters, I did observe that, for good or for bad, people really do behave differently where money is involved.

I am not sure how long it took for me to realize it, but at some point, I became aware that we were not left without greeters of our own; however, they certainly did not look like the girls I initially saw, and I was quite thankful they were not in grass skirts. Instead, our welcoming committee consisted of two men who appeared to be no more than four or five years our senior. Elder Platt and Brother Sa Ooan *(Sah OO-ahn)* introduced themselves and told us they would be taking us to the Language Training Mission (LTM) on the other side of the island, in Laie. Brother Sa Ooan was the second Thai person I had met in my life. His smile was engaging and his greeting was as sincere as anything I had ever heard in my life. He was speaking Thai, so I had no clue what he was actually saying, but he appeared truly grateful to the twelve of us for coming to his country to teach his people about Jesus Christ. Elder Platt had been back from his mission to Thailand for a year or two. We all perceived him as being much older and much more worldly-wise than I think he really was. Relative to us, though, he was a sage. He was tall and lean with black hair, and carried himself with a competent air that allowed me to immediately trust him. Throughout my two-month stay in the LTM, he never betrayed that confidence. Elder Platt was engaging but firm. For me, just right.

The first Thai I ever really talked to was Elder Sunaan *(SuNUN)*. Now there was a guy with a smile! His dark complexion seemed to act as a frame, which directed my attention to the playfulness in his eyes and the charm of his smile. He was shorter than I was but better built. (Since I was so conscious of how thin I was, I would always notice when somebody's chest and shoulders were proportioned in a reasonably manly fashion.) Elder Sunaan had been raised mostly in Thailand, but for a year or two prior to his mission, he had lived with a wealthy Mormon family in Utah. Fortunately, his English was easily understandable, though he made no attempt to hide his accent.

We loaded our bags onto a not-too-luxurious bus and began the trek around the island from Honolulu to Laie. The beaches along the way were spectacular. Everything on the island was more lush and green than anything I had experienced growing up in Southern California. We passed the snorkeling cove of Hanauma Bay and then we passed a beach where campers had set up tents in the midst of a beautiful grove of trees. What a terrific place to spend two months! As the seemingly endless stretches of beach unfolded before me, my mind turned toward how blessed I was to be engaged in missionary work in such a spectacular setting. Was this a mission or a vacation?

At the same time, I could not help but think about the things I had left behind. I had truly enjoyed my basketball season at Southern Utah State College. I regretted getting so sick on one road trip near the end of the year that I could not play in the first game of the trip against the College of Eastern Utah. Up until that time, I had started every game. I was no Pistol Pete scoring machine, but I was as tenacious a defender as anyone would want to grapple with. I fouled out of almost every game I played. Anyway, I had not told Coach Lunt about my illness until shortly before game time. I so badly wanted to play that I had hoped I would get well enough to play, and I simply did not want to say anything about how sick I was. I do not think Coach Lunt appreciated my announcement to him right before the game. I didn't start the last few games of the year and I could never think of any reason why except for being sick in Price, Utah, and not telling the coach earlier on. Despite that, I loved playing basketball, and I loved playing at Southern Utah. It was not an easy thing to give up.

I guess the other thing that occupied my mind on the drive from Honolulu to Laie, and actually throughout the course of my two-year mission, was the thought of various friends, both male and female, whom I would not be seeing for a long time. Truth be told, while thoughts of Mike Obi, Dana Duke, Mike Kan, or John Watson entered my mind, I tended more often to drift toward friends of the female persuasion and what they were up to. I hoped that I would receive letters from them all, and I particularly wondered what Debbie Van Dusen, Dara Doney, and Kathy Norris were up to.

Upon arriving at the Mormon Church's College of Hawaii in Laie, I found that the campus was located within spitting distance of the northern beaches of Oahu. Our dormitory stood to the right of the main campus. It was a fairly nondescript two-story box, which surrounded an open garden with walkways and occasional benches cutting across the grass and shrubs. The twelve missionaries destined to Thailand were all assigned to divide up three rooms on the ground level in one comer of the dormitory. Our roommates were assigned alphabetically. My previously assigned companion, Elder Roger Pace, and I were joined by a second missionary companionship, Elders John Montgomery and Robin Martell. The other eight missionaries were assigned to two other rooms, one room on each side of ours. Elder Castleton's room was separated from ours by a bathroom. This became tactically important as time went on. Someone had discovered that Elder Martell's bed was just on the other side of the wall from the toilets. Invariably, the toilet handles were tied up so that the toilets would flush nonstop, vibrating poor Elder Martell right out of his bed. It was a choice sight.

Elder Pace and I had been assigned as companions from day one in Salt Lake City. However, we had not been free to really get to know each other up to this point. All I really knew about him was that he was from Orem, Utah, reminded me of Popeye with his solid physique and square jaw line. He took life and his mission much more seriously than I did, and he had a girlfriend whom he was totally dedicated to. His plans were to return home from Thailand and marry this girl. I liked him, but I could only guess what he thought of me and my unsettled ways. My life was just not as planned out as his was.

As we crowded into our new digs, it became clear that I was not sharing space with anyone whom I would have voluntarily chosen to spend time with outside the context of a Mormon mission. At the same time, I had no illusion that the three other missionaries in the room had any different thoughts about me. Not that any of us were evil or bad fellows. Rather, our interests and tastes were just so divergent. Up to this time in my life, sports and girls had alternately dominated my mind.

By contrast, my companion had clearly gone beyond the stage of considering the various physical attributes of every woman who passed in front of him and had already settled on the one woman with whom he was to share his life. That decision having been made, he was prepared to proceed with a singleness of purpose on his missionary assignment.

Elder Montgomery seemed to view the missionary experience in Thailand as one of great adventure, not only for the missionary experiences that it would bring, but also for the adventures of life that were sure to come.

Elder Martell played the guitar, and beyond that, I never did quite figure out who he was.

I was always led to believe that my calling as a missionary in Thailand was inspired by God. God knew me and loved me and took the time to make sure I served in a mission that would be most fulfilling to me and most rewarding to those around me. While I have never been completely sure about my feelings regarding God taking the time to individually call each and every missionary to specific places of service, I am convinced the throwing together of Elders Martell, Montgomery, Pace, and Palfreyman came about solely as a result of the spellings of our last names. Regardless of how it occurred, I will forever be grateful for the fact that I was thrown in with these elders, and Elder Montgomery in particular, for my two-month LTM stay. Elder Montgomery has since become a lasting and fast friend and has enriched my life immeasurably.

Whatever illusions I might have had of my time in Hawaii being a cushy sabbatical from reality were quickly and rigorously dispelled. I was never much of a student, and in fact, still have a difficult time sitting at a desk for any longer than a few minutes at a time. I was not emotionally ready for the rigorous nature of the forced sedentary mental exercises that were required in Hawaii. The daily routine of studying Thai between eight and ten hours was absolute drudgery. My ability to focus on memorizing missionary lessons in Thai was abysmal. I constantly had to fight my wandering mind. My thoughts traveled from body surfing at the beaches at home, to basketball, to girls, and then back to the beaches.

Of course, all this unstructured daydreaming was interspersed with glimpses of the outside world in Laie, Hawaii. My dormitory window looked onto an outside basketball court. In those days, the rims were not collapsible, and the rims on these courts had been clearly mangled and abused. Still, it was on these basketball courts that two of my language instructors, Brothers Sa Ooan and Mongkon (Mone-cone), would oftentimes bedevil me by playing basketball after lights out at 10:30 p.m. The sounds of the basketball repeatedly bouncing off the asphalt, and then striking the rim under which a metal net rattled, provided me with a natural and familiar symphony of long-treasured melodies. Surely, I could not be expected to sleep under such conditions. I was constantly drawn to play and would nod off only after they finished. The upside was that the constant friendly rambling between Sa Ooan and Mongkon confirmed in my mind that I was heading to a country where the people would openly welcome my visit. Whether they would ever accept my message or not was a separate issue.

Many of our days were broken up with afternoon excursions to the soccer field where the Thailand group of missionaries would take on the elders headed for Japan. There were many more of them than us, and so we would often recruit a few of the missionaries headed to Hong Kong or South Korea to round out our team. The soccer matches were not pretty, but we were completely satisfied as we routinely beat up on the elders going to Japan. In a weird way, it became a source of pride for the Thai missionaries who were having a rather difficult time with our primary objective, which was to learn the Thai language.

Thai is a beautiful language, but not when spoken by a band of twelve nineteen-year-old boys for the first time. Words as simple as *hello (sah-what-DEE)* were amazingly difficult to master. There are five different tones that can be placed on any given syllable. Each tone can change the meaning of the word you are trying to say. The tones are as confusing to Americans as I am sure English words such as *to, too,* and *two* are to non-English-speaking people. And if the tones don't get you, then God provided the Thai people with various sounds that are not found in the English language. The best example of that is the Thai letter that would have an English equivalent spelling of *ng.* In America we can say *song* without any real trouble. Strangely, however, if you put that same *ng* at the beginning of the word, we become hopelessly confused. Try saying the word *ngu*. It means *snake* in Thai. It means utter frustration for someone trying to figure out how to speak to a whole bunch of people on the other side of the world. That was me.

Interestingly, the first few days of the LTM deceived me into thinking I was actually learning Thai at breakneck speed. Complete ignorance can often blind you to reality. I learned several individual words, and before too many days, actually began stringing together some words into phrases. I started to believe I was a regular linguist. Unfortunately, reality set in after about a week.

There were eight missionary lessons in existence at the time I went to Thailand, and we were told in Salt Lake City that we were supposed to know all eight of the lessons and their multiple concepts before we arrived in our country of service. After a week at the LTM, it became clear that was not going to happen. Indeed, the missionary lessons had not yet been fully translated into Thai, and that only extenuated the challenge. I found myself racing against time...not just to do what I had been told I must do, but simply to avoid being farther behind than anybody else in my group. Ultimately, I walked away from the LTM having learned one of the eight missionary lessons. It was little consolation that was a common achievement in my group.

As missionaries, we were somewhat isolated from the outside world. We began to rely on each other for our entertainment. At about the third week in Laie, the "Mad Puker" reared his ugly head. It was never determined who the actual Mad Puker was. His ability to surprise, and his quickness in the dormitory complex, were both significant aids in his avoiding detection. In fact, when I would hear the splat of water on the concrete doorstep, followed by the shrill shriek of one who sounded like he was at death's door, we would all jump up and try to catch this Mad Puker. But alas, he was too swift, and we were never able to positively identify the villain.

As our eight weeks progressed, the Mad Puker became ever more brave and inventive. We often wondered who among us it was that had taken on the personality of the Mad Puker and what brought it about. Was it the full moon? Maybe it was the bite of a local spider or lizard, both of which seemed to enjoy our company? Or maybe it was just the grind of a tedious day sitting at a desk trying to figure out how Thai was ever going to become a comfortable form of communication. Though I never learned the answer to any of these questions, I was always amused by the Mad Puker's visits. He was a symbol that life could have been much worse.

The tedium of the LTM was not lost on anyone. Elder Castleton, probably the most polished of the missionaries among us, was no exception. After a routinely long morning of vocabulary building and lesson memorizing, he decided to take a nap rather than eat lunch. I had become somewhat hypnotized by the monotony of the routine of things, and did not notice that Elder Castleton had not rejoined us in class after lunch. Apparently, no one else had either. While in the midst of attempting to stay consciously focused on what I was supposed to be doing, Elder Castleton waltzed into the classroom sans white shirt and tie, providing us with a wonderful sight that released a great deal of tension for me and everyone else. The ensuing laughter did not subside for some time, and when it finally did, Elder Castleton casually got up and left the room to finish getting dressed. How he could remain so dignified throughout the event was a mystery, but Elder Castleton always was able to keep his cool.

It is important to understand that as missionaries, even though we were sweating it out in the Hawaiian sun, we were required to wear slacks along with our white shirts and ties. I guess that was because this was the attire we were going to have to don in Thailand, and our leaders wanted us to get used to it. Maybe it was also a way of promoting conformity. I guess it didn't really matter anyway, as it was just the rule.

Since each of us had been to the temple, we had undertaken the commitment to wear garments at all times. As a temple-going Mormon, whether you are on a mission or not, it is expected that you wear the Mormon underwear at all times. These garments cover the body from the top of the knees to the neck, and in hot weather they can be rather stifling. (On the other hand, in the wintertime, they are quite useful.) Some believe that the temple garment constitutes a physical protection from harm and evil, while others view the garment as symbolic of the commitments made in the temple. Maybe it's a little of both.

As newly endowed elders (members who have only recently taken on the commitments required in the temple), we took very seriously the commitment to wear the garment always. It seemed even more important to maintain the integrity of the garment by never exposing it to anyone. In light of the fact that we were all newly endowed and all newly committed to the wearing of the garment and to the maintaining its sacredness through secrecy, none of us had ever experienced a lapse in our commitments.

I cannot say whether I was succeeding in focusing on language training at the time, or if I was imbibing in the somewhat frequent pastime of daydreaming when Elder Castleton came in. All I can remember is Elder Castleton entered the classroom very disheveled, eyes only half-opened, with his garment exposed for all to see. I know that whatever I was thinking about before Elder Castleton entered the room was not what I was thinking about after he took his seat. He had not yet even realized his faux pas. It was a memorable sight, one that I will never forget. Time stands still at moments like these, and so I cannot tell you if Elder Castleton sat there in all his glory for five seconds or five minutes. However long it was, the emotional outlet was invigorating.

While we mostly relied on each other for entertainment, we were allowed occasional forays into the world. The Polynesian Cultural Center was within one hundred yards of our dormitory. We could hear the constant sounds of the show's entertainment and the audience's enthusiastic reactions, but for the first three weeks in Laie, we were not privy to what was actually going on to cause all the commotion. About three weeks into our stay, we were extremely excited when told that we were going to the Polynesian Cultural Center to see the show. Now I must say that at nineteen years of age, I generally was not too excited about anything that smacked of a cultural event, but after three weeks in the LTM, it was a welcome relief to get out and see real people under any circumstances. The show was great fun. Tahitians, Māoris, Fijians, and others were all doing their native dances in their native costumes. It was such a welcome relief from the monotony of classroom style studies.

But more than the fun of the place itself, I was entranced by the people in attendance. They were regular people. None of them had white shirts on and none of them wore ties. In fact, my most memorable recollection of the afternoon was sitting by a beautiful blonde girl from Huntington Beach, California. She had just finished high school and was traveling around Hawaii for a couple of weeks before attending college. You could tell she had been in the sun, and her easy demeanor reminded me that I once had a life beyond the veil of white shirts and ties and commitments and responsibilities. It wasn't all that long ago, but it seemed like an eternity had passed.

I cannot say I was ever viewed as one of the spiritual giants among us. In fact, Elder Pace would often remind me I was lacking in spirituality. There were many nights at the LTM, as I lay down to sleep, that I felt guilty about my various lapses of attention and concentration. It was a time where I found myself trying to recommit myself to conform to what was expected of me on a daily basis. One of the mental impediments was that I could never resign myself to believe that conformity was equal to spirituality. I could believe only that conformity provided order. Order and spirituality were not necessarily the same thing. This mission, then, became a real test of my own belief system. Thankfully, there were occasional nights when I could lie down to sleep feeling satisfied that I had done my best that day.

Since I would shortly be passing the gospel message to some 38 million Thai people, telling them that Jesus Christ would provide them with a better life, it was imperative that time be spent honing my own sense of who God and His Son Jesus Christ were. One of the main ways the church attempted to assist in that quest was to provide us time to attend the temple endowment sessions. Before arriving in Hawaii, I had attended the temple three times. The first was far too new and overwhelming to provide me with any real insight into what was going on. The second two visits were the 4:00 a.m. sessions in Salt Lake I referred to earlier. As I said, they did not yield keen spiritual insight.

In Hawaii, the temple excursions we were allowed to go on provided us with time to actually try to absorb the lessons of the temple. Many doctrinal points were raised. However, I found that just as many doctrinal points were left unanswered. Ultimately, the most rewarding part of the temple involved a sense of unity of purpose that came about as a result of the commonness of the goals of all those present. Every one was dressed in white and everyone was friendly and courteous. I had the feeling of being clean and of being among friends. It was comforting and provided confirmation of purpose. I have never forgotten that. It is otherworldly in that sense.

As the time to leave the LTM neared, the thought of going became a distraction. The LTM had been quite grueling for me. My attention span was never too terrific, and this eight weeks' worth of class time pushed my attention span way beyond any bounds that it had ever gone before. But now was the time to finally venture out into the mission field, and I was anxious. The LTM had facilitated the development of friendships among my eleven companions who would help me through the hard times in Thailand. Elder Castleton was the pinnacle of confidence. Elder Montgomery was full of the sheer joy of life and infected us all with a sense of adventure. Elder Pace was single-minded, and Elder Welling was full of fun—not quite light-minded, but close.

I sought out Elder Grant Ross, who was leaving at the same time for Taiwan. He and I had been able to sneak in a few games of basketball during our eight-week stay, and I felt as close to him then as I had ever felt toward anyone else in my life up to that point. He had shared my two most exciting and defining experiences: first, my basketball days at Southern Utah; and second, my eight weeks of language training in Hawaii. (We had even switched companions on occasion to facilitate our basketball excursions in Hawaii). We said our good-byes, and it took some fifteen years before I ran across Grant Ross again.

In preparing to leave Laie, I realized I would miss seeing Elder Steve Welling sitting in the garden area of our dormitory reciting missionary lessons to his hand-drawn picture of Khun Praphan *(Koon brah-PAHN)*, a generic Thai investigator[7]. I would also miss the Mad

Puker and his nightly sorties through the dormitory. Amazingly, I would also miss Elder Platt and Brothers Sa Ooan and Mongkon, who had helped me with a lot more than just the language, including self-discipline, focus, and so forth. It was a long two months, but I had determined that I had done the best I could do given my own foibles.

III

FIRST ASSIGNMENT

After two months of agonizing over the vocabulary, sounds, and tones of the Thai language, I felt somewhat confident about my fundamental language skills, believing I would only need a brief period of adjustment before I would fit right in. In no time at all, I learned that I had substantially misjudged my level of preparedness.

Twelve white-shirted missionaries bounded off the 747 jumbo jet at the Don Muang International Airport just outside of Bangkok. Immediately after crossing the tarmack and entering the airport terminal, I was approached by a young-looking man who stood no more than 5' 3" in height and could not have weighed more than 110 pounds dripping wet. Ambling directly toward me in his khaki-green jumpsuit, it was quite apparent he was a baggage handler looking for someone to help. When he got to within five feet of me, he smiled and said, *"Sawad dii krup ben yangray bang?"*

I smiled back at him politely while mumbling, "What the heck did he say?"

Elder Sunaan, the Thai missionary in our group, either heard my somewhat muted query or saw the contorted and contrived smile I had provided to the baggage handler. Elder Sunaan came up laughing, saying, "Elder Palfreyman, he said, 'Hello, how are you?'"

I sheepishly acknowledged the greeting and turned away, concluding that my two months' worth of language training in Hawaii had been completely for naught. Fortunately, I did not have long to contemplate this small but not insignificant lesson.

On our first day in Bangkok, I was paired with an Elder Warner from Spanish Fork, Utah, who had been in the country for five months. He took me to visit some of the Thai people he was teaching in a portion of Bangkok known as Samsen *(SAHM-sane)*. Our transportation to Samsen was like climbing onto Mr. Toad's Wild Ride at Disneyland.

The gas powered, three-wheeled vehicle was no bigger than a golf cart, and our driver seemed to always be on the lookout for a checkered flag.

My first ride through a traffic circle was more than memorable as we wove our way in and out through a maze of little blue taxicabs and very large orange buses. There were only the smallest of openings in the traffic ahead of us, which our driver seemed to find great joy in exploiting, and it seemed as if it were a contest for him to get as close as possible to the vehicles through which we were negotiating our way. At times, I could have reached my hand out (and I don't mean my arm) and touched the door of a taxi, the tire of a bus next to us, or the exhaust pipe of either one.

Elder Warner got a good chuckle out of my reactions, since he had been in the country long enough to have gotten used to the life-or death nature of a typical drive through town. Over time, I must say that I, too, got to enjoy the amusement-park-like rides in Bangkok. We survived that ride to Samsen and Elder Warner paid the three-wheel driver his *five-baht* fare, which was equal to about twenty-five cents.

I was now standing in a very poor part of town. Elder Warner assured me that this was not all that bad of a neighborhood, and then we proceeded to walk. After five blocks or so, I came to be convinced that Elder Warner was correct. Where we were dropped off by the three-wheel driver was not all that bad a part of town, especially when compared to where we had walked to! Now we were in a bad part of town. Our concrete sidewalk had turned into two-inch-by-eight-inch planking laid over mud. At various places, the planking was suspended over that same mud by two or three feet. There was a gamey aroma to the mud that made me quite sure I did not want to fall off of the planking.

The housing had also changed from where we were initially dropped off. Two-story stucco apartments had given way to poorly constructed wood-sided homes, which in turn gave way to a veritable shantytown with no structure in the area standing taller than seven feet. The walls consisted of warped plywood, and roofs were consistently fashioned out of corrugated tin or fiberglass. I suppose the roofs were helpful in providing shade for those who dwelled inside, but the fact that the corrugated tin/fiberglass was previously used and full of holes, did make me wonder if the roofing materials provided any protection at all from the monsoon rains I had heard about.

My wonder did not last long, however, as I noticed that the slight slope of the corrugated tin roofs would cause water to run off the end of the roofs and into strategically placed wooden and pottery barrels. Sure enough, as I walked over and peeked into a couple of the barrels, they were full of water. The inside of each barrel was lined with green moss, and floating on top of the water was all manner of plant and animal life, some of it living and some of it dead. Elder Warner explained that these barrels provided these people with their only source of drinking water.

The people themselves in this shantytown made for quite a contrast to anything I had previously experienced. They all knew how to smile, but somehow you could tell that no joy accompanied the smiles. These people were truly living from hand to mouth. The children's clothing had not been washed in weeks, and by their appearance, I would venture to guess their bathing schedule was no more frequent. The barefooted children consistently appeared to have sunken eye sockets and a hollow, hungry, desperate look as they peered at what to them must have been oversized and overfed, white-shirted, rich Americans.

We continued our walk down the planking through the middle of this shantytown. I presumed we were simply passing through; I was wrong. In the middle of all of this poverty, filth, and stench, Elder Warner turned to me and said, "We're here."

He then pointed to one of the typically less-than-humble lean-to's. He turned toward the lean-to and negotiated the piecemeal wooden steps that had been strategically placed between the main planking and the lean-to. I was so intent on following his every step, so as not to deposit myself in the muck, that I did not see how low the gate frame was. The children who were watching got a great kick out of seeing this dumb American bang his head on the two-by-four board which was used to frame the entrance way we were passing through.

I laughed with them, consciously realizing for the first time, that I was substantially taller than any Thai I had ever met or seen. The small children chatted among themselves in the language I hoped would someday be as familiar to me as it was to them. I then heard Elder Warner speaking with someone inside the lean-to. While he was engaged in his conversation with whoever was inside, I was amused by the fact that my size, my awkwardness, and my head-banging feat were all providing a great deal of entertainment to the children in the area. By the time Elder Warner explained to me that our trip was for naught and that the member of the church we were seeking at this location was not home. By now, we had attracted quite a large crowd, young and old alike.

Elder Warner encouraged me to try to speak to the children, since that was the easiest way to learn the language. It turned out that the children were very patient/entertained by an American's lack of language skills and I have since thought this may be a universal truth...that children's expectations are limited to kindness, and if that expectation is met, then all is well. I made a mental note that adults were not so easily satisfied.

Elder Warner guided me back to the Mormon church at *soi Asoke (soy Ah-SOAK)* where my luggage had been dropped off. It was here, at the only real Mormon church house in Thailand, that I was assigned to my first missionary companion in the mission field. Elder Peckham was tall and lanky and had been in the country for three months, but by his language skills, I would have believed it if he told me he had been there for five years. You could tell by the reaction of the Thai people he spoke with that they were very impressed by his language skills. Constantly, I would hear them say, *"Chat" (chut).* I later found out that meant *clear.* It would be a long time before anyone would be saying that to me. It was a bit of a challenge for someone who only a day or two earlier was unable to decipher, *"Sawatdee krup ben yangray bang?"* from a baggage handler at the airport.

Elder Peckham helped me out to the street with my luggage, where we hailed a taxi. The taxicabs in Bangkok were not the Yellow Cab variety that I had seen one or two of in Los Angeles, California; instead, the Bangkok cabs were blue. That was not the only difference. After folding myself and my luggage into the taxi, I tried to mentally picture whether or not this Bangkok-variety taxi would actually fit inside a Yellow Cab that I had been more used to seeing. I concluded that it would be close.

This first taxi ride presented me with one of the more enjoyable tasks of a Mormon missionary in Bangkok, which is negotiating cab fare from the middle of Bangkok to the suburb of Thonburi *(TOAN-ber-ee)*. It was great fun. Missionaries were considered very poor negotiators if they paid forty *baht* (approximately two dollars). On the other hand, if you were able to negotiate a *twenty-baht* fare, you were someone to be admired. The game was played by all elders who had to traverse the distance between the church house in downtown Bangkok and Thonburi. On one occasion, some months farther into my mission, I was able to negotiate a seventeen-baht fare. Of course, this happened at about midnight, when a cabby was trying to generate his last fare of the day to Thonburi where he lived. Collecting seventeen *baht* for his drive home, he considered himself a lucky man. More significant to me, I became a legend. (Looking back, this negotiating exercise seems more cheap than Christian. Chalk this practice up to the inexperience and poor judgment of youth.)

I can hardly describe all that I saw between the church house in Bangkok and my new home in Thonburi. Bangkok was a city that was absolutely alive. Every road was choked with traffic and every car, bus, taxi, and three-wheeler had a horn that was used much more constantly than the brakes. Beautiful, modem, high-rise hotels were sandwiched in between strip-mall-like storefronts that seemed to extend endlessly down each street we traveled on. Each storefront was protected by metal gates that would completely seal off the store at closing. Bangkok appeared to me to be every bit as big as the Los Angeles I had left behind.

When we finally arrived at the *Chao Phraya (Jauw Prah-YAH)* River that separates Bangkok proper from Thonburi, I viewed a beautiful sight. The *Chao Phraya* River was nothing like the Los Angeles River. Large barges made their way up and down the muddy river and Wat Arun *(What Ah-ROON),* a landmark Buddhist temple, glistened in the noonday sun. Long and narrow needle-nosed boats quickly ferried passengers, seated two across and approximately twenty rows deep, back and forth across the river. The river seemed to have a life of its own and indeed acted as a buffer between the two parts of Bangkok.

As we drove across the bridge and into Thonburi, the buffering quality of the river became even more apparent. All of a sudden, the traffic was not quite so heavy. The pace of activity slowed down. Housing seemed somehow more suburban, and I felt like I had entered the San Gabriel Valley in Los Angeles County. Once we crossed the bridge, it only took about fifteen minutes to get to my new home.

The house was set back from the street by a good thirty to thirty-five feet, with a well-maintained lawn covering the ground in between. The stucco on the first floor was painted light green; the second floor was covered with brown wood siding, stained and varnished to maintain its natural color. Inside, on the ground floor, was a very large and spacious room that was rarely used, a bathroom, and a kitchen. The bathroom and kitchen were used exclusively by the maid, who prepared two meals a day for us. Upstairs was a large bathroom and one large bedroom. In the bedroom, four double beds stood side by side all the way across the room at one end. At the other end of the room, there were four small writing tables, one for each missionary.

Elder Peckham and I chatted while I unpacked. He was twenty years old and intended to marry his high school sweetheart, Paula. Elder Judkins, who accompanied me to Thailand from Hawaii, and Elder Gibbons, were the other two missionaries who shared our residence.

Two other missionaries also lived in the Thonburi area: Elders Heidbrink and Stratton. (The six of us formed the Thonburi District of the Thailand Bangkok Mission.) Elders Heidbrink and Stratton lived in what basically amounted to a strip mall, upstairs from an Isuzu truck dealership. Their quarters included a large room that served as a meeting hall for our church services in Thonburi.

I quickly came to realize that my reliance upon Elder Peckham was almost complete. I had no usable Thai language skills and had no clue as to where anything was, either in the house or in the city. Elder Peckham even negotiated with the maid about what we would eat on any given day. I would follow Elder Peckham around throughout each day while we ran various errands, like setting up bank accounts, going to the immigration office to fill out visa paperwork, and visiting various members.

One of the very first members I ever met was a Brother Kaaw *(Gauw)* and his family. They lived in a very small home that had no more than two rooms, but Brother Kaaw, his wife, and three children all seemed somehow to fit. He was an artist by trade; his oil paintings were favorite tourist trinkets for the missionaries. I'd never known an artist before and found it quite strange he could paint two scenes that varied only slightly from canvas to canvas. The first was of Thai thatched huts, and the second was of small barges and boats. My naivete about Brother Kaaw's artwork, I think, was the biggest reason I ultimately purchased four or five of the paintings…what I believed to be works of art that would someday be worth millions. I must have really been dreaming about Brother Kaaw's paintings and their future value when I had only paid twenty-five dollars for each one to begin with. Regardless, they were beautiful depictions of Thai scenery.

In meeting with the Kaaw family, I had my first taste of what missionary work consisted of. The Kaaws were always very happy to see me and treated me as if I was a direct messenger from Jesus Christ. Even though we had been told that was the case, it was not something I had really thought about before. But the Kaaws certainly placed me on a pedestal, along with all the other missionaries, which was terrifically ego-satisfying. Sister Kaaw routinely asked after my family and, after I had broken my ankle playing basketball, took a special interest in the state of my health.

One habit that never seemed to die was my need to play basketball. Elder Peckham immediately ingratiated himself to me forever by taking me to the local hospital the first Saturday that I was in Thonburi. There, in the middle of the complex at Sirirat *(See-ree-RAHT),* was a barely lit basketball court. The poor lighting really did not matter to me, nor did the fact that the wooden backboards did not seem capable of holding up the rims. It was this basketball court, which confirmed in my mind that Thailand was going to be a great place to work for the next two years.

My delight in seeing the basketball court was not lost on Elder Peckham, who turned to me and reported that "there are several doctors who get together here every Saturday morning and play. Would you be interested?"

I could hardly contain myself.

"We could go get our clothes and play today since it is only a couple of blocks back to the house," I eagerly responded.

Elder Peckham then slightly chastised me by reminding me, "We are on our way to a street meeting at Sanam Luang *(Sah-NAHM LOO ahng)*, and the other elders are waiting for us." Sanam Luang was an open area near the King's palace in the heart of Bangkok used for various activities including a huge weekend market (that dwarfed the flea market at the Rose Bowl in Pasadena, CA that had been my experience in the States.

There was no need for Elder Peckham to say anything more. He was right, but I sure had something to look forward to next week. All my life I had been a little punk guard trying to keep up with the big guys; here in Thailand I could be Elgin Baylor. I *was* the big guy!

"Elder Palfreyman, this is Dr. Nooy *(NOO-ee)."*

The introduction caught me off guard, compelling me to return from my fantasy of playing power forward against the smaller Thai players, whom I assumed would be putty in my hands. I turned to see a middle aged woman whose air was starkly aristocratic. On the other hand, her smile and countenance were as soft and gracious as Melanie Wilkes in *Gone with the Wind.* She introduced herself in English and from that point forward, always treated me as if we were lifelong friends.

In quite polished English, Dr. Nooy reminded Elder Peckham of our dinner appointment at her home in the coming week. I was very pleasantly surprised by the invitation and thanked Dr. Nooy, who then told me, "I look forward to getting to know you better, Elder Palfreyman. I enjoy your weekly visits." It turned out that Dr. Nooy had been having the missionaries over for dinner on a weekly basis for over a year, even though she was not a member of the church.

Sirirat Hospital was only a block away from the docks, where we boarded a ferry to cross into Bangkok. After crossing the river on the ferry and walking only a couple blocks to Sanam Luang, I beheld the most incredibly large flea market/swap meet I had ever seen in my life. I couldn't really take all of it in at first. The market was set up on an open field that stretched out at least half a mile, both to my right and to my left, directly in front of the King's Grand Palace. Elder Peckham mumbled something about not giving anything to the beggars, as I would be absolutely inundated if I gave even one *baht* (a nickel) to any of them. He then led me into the middle of the marketplace, and I was awestruck at the immensity of it all. Temporary booths were set up within which everything imaginable was being sold. All kinds of clothing, foods, household wares, and other sundries were laid out before me. None of it constituted standard American fare.

Slowly, as the vastness of the place became absorbed in my mind, I began to see more of the here and now. The small merchants were competing wildly for the attention of any and all potential patrons, but especially for the attention of the not-so-common American. After all, Thais everywhere pegged Americans in their country as fat chickens, just waiting to be plucked.

Elder Peckham guided me to a corner of the marketplace where my eyes fixed on a veritable swarm of out-of-place-looking, white-shirted missionaries. There I spied Elders Welling, Pace, and Montgomery, which made me feel as if I had come home. As I went to greet my old friends, Elder Peckham sallied up to his more senior missionary acquaintances to take care of some business.

Elder Montgomery and I exchanged pleasantries and stories of our first few days in the country, and we slowly wandered off to soak in the surroundings. Before we had ventured even a hundred yards from the other missionaries, we were warmly summoned by a street vendor selling sandals. These were certainly not of the Birkenstock variety. Instead, they were made of not-so-hardy plastic and I was sure that, as I watched the vendor twist these little toy-like sandals in his hands, he would tear them up if he was not careful. His sales pitch was heartfelt and somehow convincing, even though I did not understand a word he said. In fact, I would have bought a pair of the dumb sandals except for the fact that he didn't have any big enough to fit.

I said in English, while gesturing with my hands as if I were signing for the deaf, "Gee, you would have had a sale, but you just don't make these sandals big enough for me." Then, pointing to Elder Montgomery's feet, I continued, "But I do believe that you could find a pair for my friend."

While I know that this little Thai vendor with the warmest of smiles could not understand a single word I said, he clearly got the drift of my message. He came around his table and was kneeling at Elder Montgomery's feet with a pair of his largest sandals faster than Jerry West could get around an Elgin Baylor screen. Within a minute, Elder Montgomery walked away from that vendor, the proud owner of a *twenty-baht* (one dollar) pair of sandals.

This was a rather trivial event, but somehow bonded Elder Montgomery and me together, knowing that we were in the midst of one of the great adventures of life. Elder Montgomery looked at me laughing, and said in mock indignation, "I didn't even want these sandals!" We both laughed together as we returned to the other missionaries.

The more experienced missionaries had already begun to talk with the casual shoppers, introducing themselves as missionaries for the Church of Jesus Christ of Latter-day Saints. Elder Peckham beckoned me to join him. I was excited about finally making contact with our target audience, the Thai people, but it was also quite intimidating to think I would now finally have to begin to use what little language I knew to convince people that their lives would be better served by following Jesus Christ. After all, I wasn't even sure that I could, in a pinch, ask for the bathroom.

Elder Peckham, either seeing the trepidation in my face or remembering his own first street meeting adventure, came to me and reassured me, "All you have to do is chat, Elder Palfreyman. If you get stuck, let me know and I will come over and help you." He then handed me a dozen or so little three-fold blue brochures we called tracts and directed me out into the masses of potential converts.

Now, instead of being overwhelmed by the enormity of the weekend market at Sanam Luang, I was rocked by the seeming enormity of the task at hand. I began noticing every detail of what was going on around me. Virtually every Thai I came across was truly curious about my presence. After hearing *"sawad dee"* enough times, I got to where I could actually respond to a degree that I thought was decipherable. Then niceties such as, "How are you?" and "How much is this trinket?" quickly followed. Progress, yes, but setbacks were sure to come.

At one stand, I picked up a pair of cheap-looking sunglasses and directed my inquiry to a striking teenaged girl as to how much they were. I was rather pleased with my ability to remember the words to string together such a sentence, but the young girl's facial response to my question sent chills down my spine. I had obviously said something wrong. My only problem was that I didn't know what I had said that elicited such a horrified look on her face. I put the sunglasses down and sheepishly backed away, nodding and smiling like an idiot. Later, when I repeated to Elder Peckham what I had said, he laughed, "Well Elder Palfreyman, instead of asking her how much the sunglasses were, you told her that you had a sexual desire for her and asked her how much for her!" Those tones were as dangerous as they were frustrating to a novice to the Thai language. Appropriate apologies and an explanation followed.

The rest of the street meeting was fascinating. In a small, open part of the field, a street-show artist was monitoring a pitched battle between his pet mongoose and his cobra. I had never before seen either of these animals, and now saw firsthand what natural enemies to each the other was all about. I didn't think I would ever want to get too close to either one again. Four hours at the street meeting passed by faster than I could ever have imagined. This was to become a weekly event that I would always look forward to. In addition to having a great time and meeting lots of wonderfully friendly people, I was able to hand Elder Peckham two names and addresses of people who said they would be interested in being contacted by the missionaries for the purpose of learning about our church. I could not have had a better day, with the lone exception, that is, of propositioning that poor innocent girl.

Street meetings did not happen every day, but tracting (the practice of Mormon missionaries going from door to door in a neighborhood) did, and tracting was not much less exciting in Thailand than the street meetings. At almost every door we went to in Thonburi, we were invited in. Then, etiquette required us to eat with them. It seemed almost routine that tracting would go very slowly because at every house we had to stop and eat. Elder Peckham would introduce us, and, after some small talk, would try to turn the topic of discussion to religion. If he was successful, and he often was, he would then turn the time over to me so that I could present one of my canned sections of a certain part of the discussions I had learned in Hawaii. The Thais I spoke with were infinitely patient in enduring my pidgin Thai ... or was it simply that they were richly entertained that their language could be botched so completely by a geeky-looking white guy from the other side of the world? Anyway, tracting was an enjoyable pastime in Thailand, completely unlike the tracting I heard so much about in America, where doors were routinely slammed in missionaries' faces, but not before rude epithets were launched in the missionaries' direction.

The first couple of weeks went by very rapidly, and I began to feel acclimated to the routine. We regularly stopped by the Kaaw family's home to say hello and make sure that they knew they had friends. Being members of a Christian church in Thailand created for them the hardship of being ostracized by most of their extended family and virtually all of their friends and neighbors.

I was not used to the notion of mixing religion with government. In America, that simply isn't done except on an extremely limited basis. In Thailand, on the other hand, the Buddhist religion is inextricably commingled with the culture and government of the Thai people. Therefore, any departure by a Thai from his Buddhist heritage to the new Christian religion smacked not only of a breach of cultural protocol, but also to some was tantamount to treason. For that reason, a great deal of missionary time in Thailand was spent befriending the few members who did exist. The Kaaws were a part of what we might call a missionary's maintenance responsibilities.

The second family I met was one with whom we had Family Home Evening every Monday night. The Mormon religion includes a practice of meeting together as individual family units (usually on Monday nights) to discuss religious matters and for the purpose of bonding the individual family members together. At those Family Home Evenings, we would give a brief religious lesson ("we" meaning Elder Peckham, while I played with the kids, which did help me hone my language skills). The Manops *(Man-OAPS)* were extremely memorable to me because they always wanted to conclude the Home Evening sessions by singing. The Thai Mormon hymnal at the time was comprised of only twenty-five or so songs, that being as far as the translation process had gotten. A good third of those hymns were Christmas songs, and those happened to be the Manops's favorite songs. Every Monday night I had a very difficult time refraining from bursting out into uncontrolled laughter as we sang Christmas hymns in Thai in August.

My first chance to play basketball finally took place on a Saturday morning at Sirirat Hospital some two weeks after I was made aware of the opportunity. It was great fun playing with the doctors, nurses, and orderlies who, for the most part, were complete novices to the game. While it was not very competitive, it was extremely cordial, and I felt completely in my element. The wooden backboards turned out to be wonderful because you could really slam the ball against them with no touch at all, and as long as you had the angle right, the ball would simply die against the wooden backboard and fall perfectly into the hoop.

Our plan was to play basketball for about two hours and then head over to Sanam Luang, where we would again enjoy our routine street meeting. Unfortunately, I landed on the foot of one of the doctors, tearing up my right ankle worse than I ever had in the past. The upside was that I was already at the hospital. The doctors summoned Dr. Nooy, who I was learning was a doctor of great importance at Sirirat. She personally took charge of my care and thereafter sent me home to rest. (So as not to give this setback any more importance than it needs, I note here only that the ankle did not get better in a very prompt fashion. I was three weeks on crutches, another three weeks in a cast, and finally one full week in bed before I could return to my regular missionary work without substantial discomfort.)

After about a month, the missionary experience became rather routine. That is not to say it was dull and boring, but only that it was something I became accustomed to. Our proselyting assignment covered a very large geographic area, and Elder Peckham and I would, on a weekly basis, take a needle boat through the canal systems to an outlying neighborhood called Nonthaburi *(Noan-TAH-ber-ee)*.

These rides to Nonthaburi were always entertaining but only marginally effective in terms of looking up prospective contacts to teach. With each trip, the area became better known to the general missionary effort and the people in Nonthaburi did begin to become familiar with our presence. My enjoyment of these trips was very selfish. I loved the thatch-roofed houses that dotted the banks of the canals. I loved seeing the people do their laundry, bathe their children, and fish the canals. The canals were their lifeblood, and the people's connection to them seemed to bring them peace and contentment that the city dwellers were never able to experience. Life just seemed more peaceful up the canals in Nonthaburi.

IV

PERSONAL CONFIRMATION

As the mission conference approached, I was advised by Elder Gibbons that, among all the other rules he had been sharing with me since my arrival, a suit was required apparel. Unfortunately, my suit was still wadded up in the bottom of my suitcase, which was where I had hoped it would remain until I went home to California in two years. Elder Peckham assured me that we could simply arrive a half an hour early and have the suit coat pressed then. I didn't give it another thought until we jumped into the taxi and headed for Bangkok.

This missionary conference was to include all of the missionaries currently serving in Thailand and the mission president. The purpose of the conference was to discuss mission-wide goals, receive instructions regarding proselyting methods, and share our testimonies that included our thoughts and feelings about our work.

The conference room was rather cavernous for what I had expected to be a brief instructional meeting with a not-so-brief follow-up testimony meeting. The tables and chairs were set up in the shape of a square, one chair for each of the fifty or so missionaries, with special seating for President Paul D. Morris and his wife Betty at the head table.

After all the missionaries took their places, a report was given that the mission had conducted five baptisms in the past six months. The president's assistants, Elders Brown and Isrealson, then presented goals for increasing our efficiency, goals that I never quite heard or paid much attention to. I have always had an aversion to meetings that were meant to psyche you up to perform a task I felt I was already working pretty hard at.

Besides, if we were to experience a cheerleading exercise, I would much rather look at actual cheerleaders instead of Elders Brown and Isrealson (no offense meant). Both stood about 5' 10" with Elder Isrealson looking spit and polish. Not that there was anything wrong with Elder Brown's appearance; it's just that Elder Israelson was rather formal and Elder Brown was not. Regardless, I must say they were an impressive pair. Elder Isrealson was an absolute workhorse, a CPA type, while Elder Brown could see the humorous side of the Hindenburg disaster. Together, they were extremely effective while, at the same time, warm and personable. Their portion of the program concluded soon enough, and the testimony meeting began. Somehow, my mind was not yet focused on the conference, nor was I prepared for the moment that was to come, which would confirm the direction of my life.

One thing I will say about Mormon testimony meetings, you will rarely be in a setting where platitudes and accolades are more predictable. Growing up in the church, I have attended hundreds of testimony meetings. Each congregation engages in testimony meetings on the first Sunday of every month. It affords the members of the congregation an opportunity to extemporaneously address the entire congregation about whatever is on their minds. Such an open-ended format allows for truly spiritual thoughts on some occasions, but it also opens the door for a lot of crackpot diatribes filled with meaningless anecdotes.

On this occasion, I remember distinctly the sense that I could feel my mind and my soul drifting away from the testimony meeting itself. This was not so unusual for me in a testimony meeting. I oftentimes daydream in such meetings about the beach, basketball, or a myriad of other topics having nothing to do with the point of the meeting at hand. Here, the testimony from each missionary seemed to blend into the one that preceded it, and after a while, I lost any specific sense of what was being said at all. I don't know how much time passed from my last conscious recollection of what was going on in the meeting, and I don't know how many missionaries got up and shared their feelings before I began to experience my own personal awakening.

Physically, I was still at the conference, but emotionally and mentally, I had traveled to uncharted territory. I was struck by an absolute sense of peace and tranquility, centered directly in front of me and slightly above the level of the table. I began to feel the presence of someone who had not been there before. This feeling and sense of absolute peace continued to expand in intensity until all at once, my spiritual eyes seemed to be looking directly at Jesus Christ. I can't really explain it other than to say He was there. I remember wondering if I should reach out and touch Him. While I did not, I still feel that I could have, but that touching Him was not necessary to make the experience any more real. It was not in a physical sense that I saw Him anyway. There was never a question as to who He was or whether or not He was really there. The only question that came to my mind at the time was why? Why me? Whatever the reason, the experience confirmed for me on a personal level that Jesus Christ was real, that He approved of my efforts at the time, and that He truly cared about me.

Not a word was spoken, not a gesture made. Despite that, I have never felt a more complete sense of peace or unfeigned love either before or since.

The experience was so overwhelming that I simply have no recollection of anything about the conference from that point on. My sense of the experience is that it is so personal that even though it is extraordinary and absolute in my mind, I can never prove to anyone else that it ever happened. At the same time, no one can ever convince me that it didn't.

V

GEARING UP

One item of business that occurs at conferences involves the shifting of missionaries from place to place. I do not know exactly why this shifting is required all the time, but it is a standard practice throughout the various missions of the Mormon Church. On this occasion, such a shift brought a definite change in approach to missionary work for me. Our district leader, Elder Gibbons, was being reassigned to a new area. (A district leader is responsible for a small group of missionary companionships.) He was replaced by Elder Patterson from Bountiful, Utah. Elder Gibbons and I butted heads over rules. Looking back, Elder Gibbons, with a little more time in country, probably had a more mature approach to rules than I did. Elder Patterson, on the other hand, was very relaxed and was able to handle weekly district meetings in a quiet and relaxed manner that more aligned with my personality. Rules were not ignored, but were relegated to a less important position. Specific contacts were focused on. Methods of how to best teach using individualized approaches with previous contacts and how to meet new contacts were discussed. It was a refreshing leadership approach for me.

The first change we all agreed on was to limit attendance at our English classes to sixteen-year-olds and up. It was agreed that there was not much potential for conversions where an under-sixteen-year-old was concerned. In such cases, not only would we have to convince the youth that he or she should join the church, but we would then have to go to the parents to confirm the "sale." Such a two-pronged task was rarely completed successfully. Class sizes immediately shrunk by about half, but I was still able to meet with eight to ten people per class per week. While I was helping these Thai people speak better English, I was also improving my Thai skills and occasionally making valuable inroads with my students for future religious contacting purposes.

A second change immediately instituted by Elder Patterson was that the singing group we had slowly been trying to mold ourselves into was to be used immediately or abandoned. Up to this point, we had just practiced, never feeling all that comfortable about how good we were. (With good reason. We were terrible!)

Elder Patterson observed that, "This singing group was not put together to generate gold record albums or make millions of dollars. The purpose of the group was simply to attract a crowd so that we could teach them about Jesus Christ."

That sounded reasonable to me, but he then concluded that, "Having defined the purpose of the group, we will now begin singing at the various traffic circles in Thonburi before we begin our actual proselyting."

Such a directive scared me to death, even though it made perfect sense. I was no singer then, and I am no singer now, and I am not deaf. I could hear my own voice, but what was worse was that I could hear the voices of some of my missionary companions who were also conscripted to sing in the group.

Up to this point, our Tuesday and Thursday street meetings at the traffic circles in Thonburi were rather quiet and peaceful. That all changed the first Tuesday night we showed up with guitars and began to sing (a somewhat generous description) our various American songs, such as John Denver's "Country Roads," and Peter, Paul & Mary's "Leaving on a Jet Plane" and "500 miles." The Thais loved the music, but I am sure they could not understand a word of what we were singing. We began drawing very large crowds of people. While these street meetings were fun before we began singing at them, we began to see the street meetings turning into veritable events. People in groups of twos and threes quickly accumulated into crowds of up to fifty people at a time. We had hit upon a good thing, but being the rather inexperienced missionaries that we were, we were not quite sure what to do with it.

Our next district meeting was called to order by Elder Patterson, and after some discussion, it was agreed that large sign boards should be constructed, which would introduce our religious message to the people gathered at these street meetings. As luck or divine providence would have it, Elder Judkins was a terrific artist and Elder Peckham's Thai handwriting was almost flawless. Between them, they created three four-by-four street meeting boards, each focusing on a different specific aspect of our religious message. From that point on, our Thonburi street meetings actually became more productive while still being enjoyable.

It was at these street meetings I heard many philosophies and religious theories that I thought were occasionally interesting and oftentimes preposterous. One fellow told me that the world was flat and that attempts by various governments to make us all believe the world was round were only a part of a plot to control our movements on the surface of the world.

A Hindu man spent a great deal of time thanking me for coming to Thailand to try to educate the Buddhist populace (ninety-seven percent of Thailand is Buddhist). He then chided me somewhat for trying to convert the Buddhists to Christianity, rather than the proper religious philosophy, Hinduism. When asking him what the basic tenets of Hinduism really were, I was given an example of reincarnation. This fellow explained, "My mother passed away a of couple years ago, but we found her in the next province reincarnated as a cow."

I asked, "How do you know that that particular cow is your mother?"

"She told me," he insisted.

In my mind, I was wondering if he was simply playing with me or if he was serious, so I then asked, "Do you speak with her often?"

He responded, "I visit with my mother often. At least once a month."

With that, I invited myself to travel with him on his next visit to see his mother. I jotted down my name and address so he could swing by and pick me up. Unfortunately, I never heard from him again.

I always enjoyed the street meetings. I met lots of quirky people, like my flat-earth theorist and my Hindu friend. There was something about the hustle and bustle associated with the street meetings that seemed to release me from my insecurities about being little more than a juvenile telling people, who had much more life experience than me, how they should alter their lifestyles according to the teachings that I was willing to impart to them. I soon learned that not all crowds would give me this sense of freedom and security.

VI

REVOLUTION

I t was on October 13, 1973 that Elder Peckham and I learned that Spiro Agnew was no longer Richard M. Nixon's vice president and that a new Vice President of the United States had been named. While it did not seem to directly affect our lives in any particular way, Elder Peckham and I felt compelled to walk down to the newsstand at the docks in Thonburi to read about our new vice president. As we approached the newsstand at the docks, I observed approximately the same number of people who always frequented the area hustling and bustling back and forth, trading fresh fruits and fish, and soliciting riders for their taxis and buyers for their sundries. I could not help but also note that there seemed to be an edge to the people on this particular day.

They were not quite as relaxed and friendly as they normally were.

Elder Peckham and I jointly put down our three *baht* (fifteen cents) and began to read in the *Bangkok Post* (an English-language newspaper) about Vice President Gerald Ford. I had never heard of him. While we were engrossed in our reading, I became aware of a particularly striking popping sound coming from across the *Chao Phraya* River and asked Elder Peckham if he heard the same thing.

"I do," he responded. "It sounds like fireworks. They must be celebrating some holiday."

I listened a while longer as the popping sounds began to grow and observed, "The sounds of the firecrackers and barrel bombs that I remember firing off at home would never have carried all the way across the *Chao Phraya* River from the Bangkok side at Thammasat *(TUM-ah saht)* University to the Thonburi side. It sounds more like gunfire."

We then continued reading about Gerald Ford and his background as a football player and congressman. I wondered how being a football player had prepared him to be a congressman and now vice president. The importance of Gerald Ford's appointment to the vice presidency held our interest for only the few minutes it took to read the article about him. Elder Peckham and I finished reading, looked at each other, and shrugged as if the changing of the guard from Spiro Agnew to Gerald Ford was really far less interesting than we had initially supposed.

As I tucked the *Bangkok Post* under my arm, I looked around and observed a great deal of commotion. The Thais on the docks had become highly agitated. I looked beyond the docks and out onto the river. A veritable armada of boats was headed right at us from across the river at Thammasat University. This event seemed far more intriguing than the news of America's new vice president. Elder Peckham and I walked down onto the docks to await the approaching boats. The ferries and needle boats and even some junks were approaching as fast as I had ever seen any of them travel in the past. Elder Peckham and I had no clue what was going on. As the boats got closer, I observed they were crowded with people, and that as they finally came alongside the docks, the people on the boats were frightened. They were shouting, "It has begun! The revolution has begun!"

The dock quickly filled with people and Elder Peckham exclaimed, "We'd better get out of here; this does not sound good!"

I stood there, fascinated. I had not heard of any revolution or any potential for one. The popping sounds we heard coming from across the river were actually the sounds of automatic weapons fire. That sound continued, but seemed far more alive now that I understood what it was. I had stumbled upon a real live revolution. The sounds steadily grew toward a fever pitch. The people around us were panicked. Several began to tell us we should go home since the soldiers would be coming shortly.

While the whole event was very exciting—I mean, it is not every day that you get to observe the beginnings of a revolution—I began to get the sense that Elder Peckham, and those several Thais around us who were advising us to go home, were right and that we should leave. Elder Peckham and I finally turned away from the river to head home, but the path had already become blocked. Thousands of people had streamed onto the streets, yelling and screaming at the tops of their lungs. The air was absolutely charged. People continued to go out of their way to warn, "This is not your fight; get home before you get hurt!"

Elder Peckham and I inched our way up the docks and toward the street so that we could go home. Progress through the crowd was virtually impossible. I remember one mother in particular crying for her son, who was at Thammasat University across the river. She was sure he had already been killed. Several students were trying to get down to the boats to cross back over the river to join their comrades, but there were no boat captains willing to return to the Bangkok side of the river.

After fifteen or twenty minutes of trying to push our way through the crowd, we finally arrived at the front of Siriraj Hospital, which was only a block or so from the docks. I watched as an olive-drab Volkswagen bus tried to force its way through the crowd and into the hospital. As that vehicle passed in front of me, I witnessed bodies stacked on top of each other inside the van and could only hope that the driver could negotiate his way onto the hospital grounds in time to save some of those people. I could see the back of the van and I realized there was not much hope for those stacked inside. Blood was literally running down the back of the van and onto the street. It was a sight I will always carry with me.

The utter chaos of this situation brought out my more selfish side. The sight of that Volkswagen van triggered my adrenal glands into action. I became a rather strong individual, capable of moving several people at a time out of my way so that I could get out of the crowd and back to my house. Elder Peckham was no more than a step or two behind me.

Once at home, we immediately wondered to each other what was really going on. The other two missionaries in our home had never left that day, and we filled them in on what was happening.

Shortly thereafter, we received a telephone call from President Morris who advised us that the students at Thammasat University, in conjunction with other political elements in Bangkok, had begun a revolution against the military regime and that we were essentially smack dab in the middle of the fighting. He then told us to stay in the house until the fighting died down.

In the next hour or two, the four of us sat in our living room, entranced by the sound of continuing automatic weapons fire. Not much was said except maybe a few quiet and private prayers. As evening approached and the sun took its daily position between two tall palm trees in the front of our property, a knock came at our front door. It was rare in those days that anyone would come to see the missionaries, and therefore, the knock was a bit unnerving. Upon opening the front door, I was greeted in a rather abrupt manner by a Brother Chayrod (*Chai ROAD*). We had first met Brother Chayrod at one of our street meetings, and he was a current investigator with whom we were meeting on a weekly basis. He invited himself in, sat down on the couch for a moment, then stood back up, and paced nervously back and forth across the living room floor. His eyes were wide open and he looked as if he had seen a ghost.

He began, "I am glad you are all here. The revolution has begun and you will not be safe outside for some time to come!"

Brother Chayrod was a student of political science at Thammasat University at the time and apparently was an active participant in the revolution. He explained that he and several of his classmates were protesting the existence of the current military government when they were attacked by the military and the police. He described watching several of his friends being shot and killed. He then forcefully told us that the students had retaliated by burning down the police headquarters.

Over the next few days, Brother Chayrod would come to our home every evening, and report to us the events of the day. His tales of bravery and heroism (or lunacy and ignorance, depending upon which side you took) were heartrending, and at the same time, riveting. When the police headquarters was attacked, the students had to cross a small bridge. Brother Chayrod left several of his friends dead on that bridge, along with many others, before the revolutionaries were successful in finally crossing the bridge and overtaking police headquarters. He related instances where female students stood between the revolutionaries and military and their police allies, trying to stop the violence. Their reward was death.

We feared for Brother Chayrod, his friends, and all the members we knew and contacts we had made in Thonburi.

In those ensuing days, while tanks passed near our house, we could not help but wonder how many of our brothers and sisters in the church had perished in the fighting.

Three or four days passed, and it was over. I never heard much in the way of tank fire or heavy artillery fire. It was as if the military and the police both were not willing to annihilate their own people in this revolution. Instead, the military regime simply announced they were ready and willing, after this clear showing of a specific desire for democracy, to allow the great experiment of democracy to proceed. The fighting was at once over and a great sense of relief could be felt everywhere.

Brother Chayrod survived, as did everyone we had become acquainted with in Thonburi. But as we ventured out of the house and into the streets, we realized not everyone was as fortunate as we were. In front of the Siriraj Hospital stood a large billboard shrouded in black. As best as we could make out, the billboard contained the names of those who had died at the hospital. I did not stop to count how many names there were on that large yellow billboard with black handwriting, but it easily exceeded one hundred. I wondered how many more dead and missing there really were. The news reports in town pegged the total at about a thousand.

Interestingly, a week or so later, my weekly review of an international news magazine turned up a brief, one-column report of the revolution saying that only sixty-seven or so people had died. My trust in news reporting was never the same after that.

I cannot remember the excuse we gave each other for needing to go into Bangkok right after the revolution, but our curiosity was insatiable. We told the taxi driver to simply drive us around and show us what had happened. Burned-out cars and buildings were everywhere. We had him take us to police headquarters, where we drove over the bridge that had been described to us by Brother Chayrod as the path used by the students to lay siege on the police headquarters. Charred vehicles, blood stains, and chip marks in the concrete where bullets had glanced off the walls were all that remained to provide evidence of the fighting that had gone on just days before, except of course for the burned-out remains of the police headquarters.

Life got back to normal in Thonburi within a few days for us, but the people did not seem to recover so quickly. Brother Chayrod was probably the best example. His keen interest in things religious had abruptly disappeared. He seemed completely immersed in the massiveness of his experience in the revolution. He was no more than a boy, eighteen or nineteen years old, who had at once been required to experience life as even mature adults should never have to. There was a distance in his eyes and a hollowness in his voice. I am not sure that Brother Chayrod ever really recovered from those few eventful days, even though he had fought on the prevailing side and was physically unscathed. While the cause may have gone forward, I could not decide whether Brother Chayrod had really won or lost.

In the days following the revolution, normalcy was problematic. There was no more fighting to be sure, but the police had all disappeared and for a while there was no real government. Instead, young Boy Scouts could be seen out directing traffic. This clearly was an exercise in utter futility; even when the police were around, traffic was an absolute nightmare.

I noticed that the thousands of fireflies hovering around the trees at our house were going about their usual activities as if nothing had ever happened. The world had survived human interference, and not long after that, I did get the sense that life was returning to its pre-revolutionary state.

VII

SINGING

The religious life of a missionary can get rather dull for a nineteen-year-old boy. Elder Judkins was just the kind of roommate that I needed. Pillow fights with him were constant, vigorous, and always ended with a trip to the market for a Foremost ice cream. In addition to horseplay and ice cream, we also both had become fanciers of Thai postage stamps. At every opportunity, we would stop at the local post office and try to find the most unusual commemorative stamps available.

In addition to all that, we shared something of a love-hate association with the singing group that had slowly been evolving in Thonburi. There were times when "One Tin Soldier" would sound okay; there were other times when it was a dismal failure. Elder Judkins and I would ride high and sing praises when the songs began to get better. However, if the performances were not too hot, we both could have just as easily never sung another song in public again. The only thing we could not argue about was that the group certainly provided an entrée for us to meet with people whom we otherwise would never have run across.

The musical group seemed to crawl along adequately until the arrival of Elder Davies. Here, finally, was a missionary who really knew music. At once, the group began to get better and we enjoyed meeting many people through Elder Davies's good work.

Elder Davies gave us direction both in terms of how to arrange the music and how to stage our presentation. He also added missionaries from Bangkok who could really sing. Ultimately, I disappeared from the actual singing group, which was one of the better accomplishments of Elder Davies's efforts.

Later, the singing group became so successful that it aired on national television rather than just being featured at the small schoolyard venues that we were limited to when I participated. Overall, Elder Davies and his more talented music comrades were able to project the Church's image in a positive way throughout the country. This was something we had never dreamed of when we first started the group. In fact, I don't think that a single member of the original group participated in the more polished televised productions.

VIII

AMERICAN HOLIDAYS

Elder Pace put together a spook alley at the Mormon church-house in Bangkok at Halloween time that was small by American standards, but absolutely hair-raising to Thais who had never heard of Halloween before. Bodies rising out of coffins, surprise visits from ghosts and goblins, flashing strobe lights, and eerie sounds had many Thais literally crawling by the time they came to the last section of the spook alley, where Elder Judkins and I had set up a meat grinder with well-placed hamburger and ketchup. I had tied up Elder Judkins's arm behind his back and made it look as though I was grinding his arm through the meat grinder. I suppose at this point, it is important to say that a spook alley on Halloween has virtually nothing to do with the Mormon Church. On the other hand, it was quite a terrific way to attract several hundred Thais to the Mormon Church so that we could say hello and introduce ourselves.

Member outings to the roller skating rink and bowling alley were other means of creating levels of comfort between the missionaries and the members and investigators.

Near the end of my stay in Thonburi, just before Christmas, I felt the air begin to take on a chill. Up to December, the heat and humidity were absolutely unrelenting. Showers seemed almost useless, for as soon as I toweled off from one shower, I felt as if I needed another. Speaking of showers, they were unlike anything I had ever seen before. Showers in Thailand consisted of a hose connected to a small heater. Both were attached at about eye level to one wall of the bathroom. You could stand in front of the contraption that was called a shower, or you could remove the hose from the wall and extend it to the sink, where you could shower while you were shaving or brushing your teeth. The ultimate benefit, though, was that you could stretch the hose all the way across the bathroom and actually shower while you were sitting on the toilet. Now there's convenience for you. In fact, it was perfect for my broken ankle days. The drain for the shower was simply placed in the middle of the bathroom floor.

Thonburi was a wonderful place to work. It was the residence of one of the most inspirational members of the church I have ever met…Brother Mani *(Mah-NEE)*. Brother Mani was a recent convert to the church who was dedicated to helping the missionaries meet and teach the Thai people of Thonburi, and his sincerity was absolutely heavenly. You heard it in every word he spoke, and you could read it in his puppy-dog eyes. He truly was without guile. One fine evening, Brother Mani joined us at a street meeting at a traffic circle in Thonburi. We had been there for about an hour doing what we always did. By now, my language skills allowed me to actually speak with passersby on my own for rather extended periods of time. Hence, I had become much more independent.

While engaging one gentleman in the usual banter, I heard an extremely loud voice shouting words that I had never heard before. It was unnecessary for me to know the precise meaning of the words, as the tone of the voice told me that someone was in trouble. I turned toward the other missionaries to see an eighteen- to twenty-one-year-old man screaming and yelling at Brother Mani. I could not believe my eyes. Brother Mani was being pushed across the traffic circle and being spit upon as if he were less than human. This young man was shouting, "By associating with this *farang ki nok,* you are no longer a Thai. You have disgraced your country and you are nothing more than a traitor."

The phrase "farang ki nok" *(fah-RAHNG kee nok)* is a favorite Thai term of derision meaning "American bird shit." Similar epithets followed for what seemed like an eternity. Ultimately, other Thais in the area came and grabbed hold of the malcontent and pulled him away. Brother Mani was in tears. All he could say was, "I am proud to be a Thai and I am proud to be a Christian."

A second gentleman came up to Elder Montgomery and began to push and shove him, and accuse him, saying, "You are trying to take our heritage from us. Go home; we don't want you; go home!"

With that, several people came to Elder Montgomery's aid, fought off the interloper, and proudly exclaimed, "We are Thai! We are free!

We have just fought a revolution so that people can think and say what they believe! You are welcome here. Don't leave because of this."

That night, I thought long and hard about what Brother Mani was all about. I had grown up in the church in California, where there was very little open hostility toward Mormons. I had never before seen the kind of overt bigotry and hatred which rained down on Brother Mani that night. I truly feared for his safety. He did not.

He was meek, and yet firm at the same time. He stood his ground. "I am Thai and I am Christian."

While I liked Brother Mani before, he became a hero to me on that night, and I loved him for his strength of character.

Periodically, missionaries are moved from city to city pursuant to the prerogative of the mission president. One of the mission president's biggest jobs is to coordinate the placement of missionaries based upon mission needs, missionary language skills, and experience. It was time for such moves again, and after four months in Thonburi, I had been reassigned to the north country in Lumphoon *(Lum-POON)*.

Immediately after finding out about the moves, I went to Dr. Nooy. She and her husband had been extremely kind and hospitable during my stay. She would never become a Mormon, but in many ways had willingly helped the missionary effort in Thailand. We were always able to take our own maladies to her for diagnosis and care. On several occasions, we took members to her as well. She generously treated all who came and never asked for anything in return. Her husband was an important businessman in Bangkok and president of the Lyons Club for all of Thailand. And though he was very busy and a high-profile community leader, he never hesitated to take time out to make sure that all was well with us.

I realized early on that I could never make them better people than they already were. It created a dilemma for me. Did they have to become Mormons to be saved in Jesus Christ? Wouldn't their resurrection provide them with the requisite knowledge of Jesus Christ? And, even more to the point, did they have to be Mormons within the broader context of Christianity? Better people I would never meet.

I said my good-byes to Dr. Nooy and her husband, and left. As we walked home, I could only think of how sad it was that my assignment would now take me away from these fine people.

As it turned out, I did have an opportunity to see Dr. Nooy one more time. A couple of days before I was to leave for Lumphoon, I came down with something called "dengue fever." Apparently, it comes from a mosquito bite, but all I knew was that by the time it fully hit me, I was reduced to a bag of bones lying on my bed without the ability to even raise my fingers off the mattress or turn my head from one side to the other. The other elders literally carried me to the hospital, where Dr. Nooy happily took care of me one more time.

IX

LUMPHOON

I was told it would be cold in Lumphoon and that I should accumulate blankets and some warm clothing, since I would be arriving in Lumphoon in the middle of the cold season. I took the advice lightly, asking, "How cold could it be?"

Bangkok was routinely in the nineties, with humidity at about the same level. Even if Lumphoon was twenty to thirty degrees colder, it would still be hot. I soon learned that once the Bangkok heat and humidity have thinned your blood, the thermometer does not have to drop all that far to chill you to the very bone.

By the time I arrived in Lumphoon, I was wishing I had paid attention to all the elders who had told me to stock up on warm clothing and blankets. Cold and hot are truly relative terms. The coldest it ever got in Lumphoon was probably about thirty-two degrees Fahrenheit. But compared to the ninety-five-degree temperatures with ninety-nine percent humidity I experienced in Bangkok, Lumphoon was a veritable icebox.

The house in Lumphoon was actually one of the nicer homes in town. Even so, as I lay in bed that first night, I was able to see the great outdoors through the vertical slats of the house's warped, wood siding, which was the only thing to come between me and the cold night air with the exception of my flimsy blanket. I was not sure I would like the idea of spending much time in Lumphoon, where I could lie in my bed and watch my breath seemingly turn to frost before my eyes every time I exhaled. First thing the next morning, I purchased a thick, warm blue-and-white-checkered blanket that became a treasure to me and has accompanied me throughout my life since then, until my wife practically gave it away at a garage sale when we moved from South Pasadena to Laguna Beach, CA.

Lumphoon was a beautiful rural town of about six thousand people, surrounded by orchards of *lumyai (LUM-yai)* trees and rice paddies. Elder Kirby and I rode thick-wheeled, tank-like bicycles around town for transportation and tended to spend a substantial amount of time shooting the breeze with merchants and other casual passersby. The pace of life was decidedly slower than what I had experienced in Thonburi.

The biggest contrast between my first companion, Elder Peckham, and Elder Kirby, my new companion in Lumphoon, was probably the pace of their own lives. Elder Peckham had come from Salt Lake City, Utah, which was like Gotham City compared to Hyrum, Utah, Elder Kirby's hometown. Otherwise, they were quite similar. Elder Peckham was in love with his high school sweetheart Paula, who was keeping tabs on him through the traditional weekly letter-writing campaign, while Elder Kirby had already become engaged to his high school sweetheart Jean. (Elder Kirby actually carried architectural drawings for his dream home with Jean). They were both very good with the language. Elder Peckham spoke Thai beautifully, constantly receiving praise as to how clearly he spoke; Elder Kirby's expertise was his vocabulary and reading prowess. It turned out that I was a lucky missionary. My LTM companion and my first two in-country companions were all kind, friendly, and easy to get along with. Not all missionaries have such good fortune.

Both Elders Peckham and Kirby did tend to drive me a little crazy by their incessant ruminations about their girlfriends. I felt like I knew both Paula and Jean, even though I had never met them. In both cases, I wondered if the girls would be gone by the time my companions went home from Thailand. It just did not seem right to embark on that most committed form of lifestyle (marriage) so soon after a mission. I have no idea why I felt that way, but I did.

The days in Lumphoon were very relaxed in contrast to the constant motion of things in Bangkok. Each morning as the sun's rays streamed through our window (and through the slats in our walls), I would poke my head out from under my blue-and-white-checkered blanket and marvel that it was cold enough in my room to see my breath. I have never been an efficient morning riser, and the weather did not help. Elder Kirby would always beat me into the only bathroom in the house.

It was too cold for me to simply lie in bed once I was awake, and I couldn't use my usual crutch of a shower to help wake me up. The only remaining alternative that I could come up with was to exercise. My father had previously sent me a regimen of Royal Canadian Air Force exercises, and for the first time in my life, I began in earnest to consistently exercise. It was awful. Not that the exercises were difficult; they weren't. It was just a consistently dull and time-consuming task. I often thought how wonderful it would have been to have a television set to watch while I exercised. Instead, it would usually take me fifteen minutes or so to get out of bed after

Elder Kirby had already gone into the shower. Then I would have to rise quickly from under my treasured blanket, and rigorously proceed through my exercises at breakneck speed, so that I could time my entrance into the shower precisely when Elder Kirby emerged.

Many of our mornings were spent tracting various parts of town. Being in a rural setting, we would slowly make our way through one neighborhood after another, keeping track of where we had been so that we would not repeat tracting in the same neighborhood twice. Before I got to Lumphoon, Elder Kirby had made contact with two or three people whom he was in the process of teaching. He also had begun teaching English at a couple of schools and at the only hospital in the province. It didn't take very long before I realized that we were actually teaching more discussions and lessons than I had ever taught in Thonburi.

As we proceeded, I noticed that I was beginning to carry on conversations with our contacts and other people. The language barrier was beginning to noticeably fall.

The nights came early and were definitely cold, so we had gotten into the routine of simply bundling up after dark, and studying scriptures or the new Thai language missionary discussions. I have never been much for sitting around and studying anything. My childlike (or was it childish?) attention span simply did not allow for it. One early evening, as I paced back and forth across the bedroom floor wrapped in my blanket, I looked out the window and noticed a crowd of men gathered around a trash can. The contents of the trash can had been lit on fire, and it looked as if they were warmer outside around the fire than I was inside in my blanket. I thought about how I could join those gentlemen and tried my approach on Elder Kirby. "Look at all those guys standing around that trash can. It is almost as if we have a captive audience to introduce ourselves to and to practice my Thai on."

My strategy of appealing to Elder Kirby's quest to provide me with opportunities to practice my language skills worked. Of course, it may also have been that Elder Kirby was also freezing and wanted to get closer to that fire. Either way, our tradition of seeking out burning refuse in the evenings in Lumphoon began. The smell of burning refuse including lots of plastic, though putrid to most, is invigorating to me to this day.

It was great fun talking to the local neighborhood chaps who told stories to support their claim that this was the coldest cold season they could ever remember in Lumphoon. Just as often, they talked about their rice crops and lumyai orchards. Not infrequently, one or two of their numbers had imbibed a sufficient amount of Thai beer to free them up to discuss the topic of religion with us. It was in this setting that I first began to understand both the depth and the hollowness of the phrase, "All religions teach man to be good."

The phrase at once welcomed us as purveyors of religion in their country while simultaneously dismissing any requirement on their part to compare their religion to Christianity...it really didn't matter since both taught men to be good. While I initially found the phrase cute, I learned to hate it as the ultimate cop-out.

Elder Kirby and I met a man named Piichion *(PEE-chee-ahn)* on one of our evenings out. He was a delightful single man who was interested in our message, more out of cultural curiosity than out of religious curiosity, as it turned out. Regardless, he cordially invited us to teach him on several occasions. Following one such occasion, Piichion explained to us that he would be spending the next week or two along the Thai-Burmese border. It turned out that he was a heavy equipment operator, and he was assigned to do roadwork along the border in the middle of the Golden Triangle. Heroin was the "gold" in the Golden Triangle, with communist insurgents, bandits, and every other type of rogue you could think of trying to cash in. Consequently, it was not the safest place to visit, but it was intriguing.

"Why don't you come with me on my next trip?" he asked. I excitedly responded, "We would love to."

Piichion then said, "I will arrange things."

All the way home, Elder Kirby chastised me for agreeing to travel outside of our assigned proselyting area. I responded by encouraging Elder Kirby to simply: "ask President Morris." If he approved of such an excursion, then we would not be violating any rules. To my delight, Elder Kirby agreed.

There were no members of the church in Lumphoon besides Elder Kirby and me. However, one member did live in the small village of Ban Sang *(Bah-SAHNG)*, approximately one hour south of Lumphoon by bus. Her name was Sister Nariphon *(NAH-ree-pahn)*. She had been converted to Christianity by way of the Mormon Church in Bangkok while studying at the university. She was very friendly and accommodating to our needs, though she was not the most regular attender I had ever seen. Still, it was nice to have at least one member whom we could occasionally see. It was rather dull to hold church services and have only Elder Kirby to look at. It seemed even more strange to bless and pass the sacrament to only the two of us. In those days, it was extremely gratifying when Sister Nariphon or some investigator would show up to our church services, which were held in the living room of our home.

X

SURGERY

Recreationally, Elder Kirby and I had found the local basketball team and had begun playing with them on a regular basis. We were very definitely a curious sight to the Thai players, many of whom had never met an American before. It always seemed gratifying to me that my being in Thailand and meeting so many people was, in itself, a service. Walls of suspicion, mistrust, and ignorance were routinely lowered as they out-hustled me for a loose ball or suffered the consequences of my pointy elbows crashing down on top of their heads after grabbing a rebound. I do not know that I could ever articulate how comfortable and at home I felt when I played ball.

One of the new assistants to President Morris, Elder Simmons, had previously spent some time with me when I was in Thonburi. He was about as wide as he was tall and had been an all-state high school wrestler in Idaho, I seem to recall. His chest was so large and bulky that he was often asked by Thais why he had breasts and was a man.

Elder Simmons was about as good-natured as you could imagine and never took offense. He would just laugh uproariously at the observation and then would respond in English with comments such as, "How can your mother love such a dirty child? You really need a bath." With his amicable smile, they always took his comments as being great compliments. He was always a favorite with the Thai people.

Be that as it may, Elder Simmons was assigned to test my language skills by listening to my presentation of one of the discussions. I never enjoyed being put on the spot. My hands became cold and clammy and I began to sweat, even though it was the middle of the cold season. We were seated on the deck upstairs at the house, and I remember getting no more than two or three sentences into the discussion when Elder Simmons eased my mind as much or more rapidly than had ever been accomplished before. He climbed up onto his chair, crouched down low, and swung his arms back and forth, chanting like an ape. The children in front of our house began to gather around and watch. He became more and more animated, scratching the top of his head and under his arms. Elder Simmons danced from chair to chair, and I soon forgot how nervous I believed I should have been. That was the first and last language test I experienced in Thailand. I am not sure whether or not God intervened on my behalf in this instance, but I like to give Him credit for the help anyway.

Early on in my stay in Lumphoon, my longstanding groin pain began to get worse. After a month or so, I had been reduced to walking around town with both hands in my pockets, keeping my fingers over the holes in my abdominal wall so as to keep my guts from slipping out. I hated when that would happen. The assistants to the president came to visit us in Lumphoon and ordered me to see a doctor in Chiang Mai *(Chee-ANG Mai)*, a beautiful province just north of Lumphoon. One of the assistants, Elder Hallows, accompanied me as my temporary companion. (We were never to be without a companion.)

The doctor looked me over for no more than a minute, groping around my unmentionables, asking me to turn my head and cough. (This was a Wednesday.) He looked at me and assured me, "This is no emergency. You don't need hernia surgery immediately. You can come back on Friday if you would like."

Elder Hallows then asked the doctor if I could travel to Bangkok for the surgery. Happily for me, the doctor agreed.

Arrangements were quickly made for me to travel back to Lumphoon and pack a bag so that I could go with the assistants to Bangkok for the surgery. I remember feeling that I had no time to prepare for this. My hernia problems had accompanied me from the States, and I had preferred to take them back with me. The idea of surgery in Thailand was not something I liked thinking about. Unfortunately for me, the doctor, the APES (a nickname for the assistants to the president), and President Morris all agreed: the surgery should go forward. I just wished it could have been one of their groins instead of mine.

The decision to submit me to bilateral inguinal hernia surgery had been made. The trick now was to get me to Bangkok as quickly as possible. The last train out of Lumphoon to Bangkok would be leaving in two hours, which gave me fifteen minutes to pack, since we happened to be in Chiang Mai.

I had never been operated on before, and, in fact, I had never even had any kind of a major injury or illness that placed me totally in the hands of someone else. I was not a happy camper. As soon as I got to the Lumphoon house at 12 Sanbayang *(Sun-buy-YANG)*

Road, I ran upstairs and packed what I needed for the trip. Just before running back down the stairs, I took a brief moment to kneel at my bedside and ask for God's help. Time limitations as they were, I could only say, "Dear God, I am scared to death. Be with me and see me through this. In the name of Jesus Christ, amen."

I simply didn't have time to explain the whole situation to God. I hoped that He would understand. I jumped up from the bed and ambled down the stairs with my bag. I was immediately on my way to Bangkok. The train ride to Bangkok from Chiang Mai took all night, and the chickens and other livestock that accompanied us did not make for a peaceful night's rest. Regardless, we arrived in Bangkok at about 8:30 a.m. and reported to the mission office. After I advised President Morris that I felt okay, he allowed me to travel over to Thonburi and work with the missionaries for a couple of days. My pre-operative appointment with the surgeon was scheduled for Monday.

In Thonburi, I was reunited with my first companion, Elder Peckham, and the other two members of my first district, Elders Judkins and Patterson. It was great to go tracting in the old neighborhoods again, and to go back to the familiar traffic circle, where I had participated in so many prior street meetings. In just a month, my language had improved to the point where I actually could speak with the passersby without interpretive help from Elder Peckham. I was pleased that he was impressed. It was gratifying that my senior training companion took pride in the progress of his trainee.

The next day, I was advised that the Bangkok missionaries were having one of their proselyting-type basketball games scheduled at a local trade school. I, of course, wanted to play, and every missionary present had to swear that the mission president's wife, Betty, could not be told of my participation. She was responsible for the missionaries' well being and would have had a heart attack if she knew that I was playing on the eve of surgery. But the heart attack would not have come before she had wrung every one of our necks. I must admit that I always felt that even if she wasn't responsible for our well-being, she would have looked after our interests anyway. With four boys of her own, it seemed that taking care of us had become a part of who she was.

The way the game was set up, seven elders could play in the game, while five more elders would circulate through the ranks of the spectators, introducing themselves and the message of our Christian faith. My yellow jersey bore the number "10," the same number I wore in both high school and college. My name was spelled out in Thai letters over the top of the number on the back of the uniform.

The sky was blue and the weather warm (unlike Lumphoon) and I was playing basketball. Life couldn't get much better. I would like to say that we lost that game as a goodwill gesture, but we didn't. Still, it was great fun. The next morning, we arose early and, it being Saturday, proceeded to Sanam Luang where we all participated in the by-then traditional street meeting. I had missed the hustle and bustle of Bangkok and the camaraderie of so many missionaries.

I attended church on Sunday, and then spent that afternoon studying Thai vocabulary words, which I had never dreamed I would have needed to know. Words for *bilateral inguinal hernia, recovery time, anesthesia,* and the like were all placed on a fairly long list that I pocketed in preparation for my meeting with the doctor the next morning.

I arrived at my doctor's appointment early and was shepherded into an examination room almost immediately. Before I could even pull out my vocabulary list, the doctor waltzed into the room with an out stretched hand and as friendly as could be, said, "Hi, how 'ya doin'?"

This Thai doctor spoke better English than I did. It turned out that he had studied medicine at Ohio State University after having graduated from college at another American university. I didn't have to look at any of my Thai medical terms. That was a wonderful relief. The evaluation lasted less than ten minutes, and I was then given the rest of the day to work around the mission office.

I reported to the French hospital in Bangkok early Tuesday morning and was shown to my room. I changed into one of those idiotic backless hospital gowns that apparently are the universal garb throughout the world in the hospital business. As I laid in bed waiting for the next step in the process, I thought about what a break it was to not have to eat fried rice for a couple of days. I was actually looking forward to hospital food for a change.

As that pleasant thought floated through my mind, an absolutely stunning nurse came through the door, pushing a cart ahead of her. This nurse should have been on magazine covers rather than teasing patients in a hospital. On top of the cart, I noticed shaving cream, a razor, and a hypodermic needle. I immediately panicked. There was no way I could allow a woman who looked like she did shave my private parts in preparation for surgery. After all, I was on a mission and simply did not have that kind of self-control. As I tried to figure out how I was supposed to keep blood in my toes and in my brain and out of other body parts, she came up alongside of me and smiled. She then began to fumble around with the cart and the items thereon.

I sheepishly tried to make conversation by saying, "Hello, ma'am, how are you?"

She was pleasantly surprised that I had addressed her in Thai and immediately began to talk to me as if we were old friends. Now I felt even more uncomfortable about what I believed she was about to do to me. Christians believe that God will not tempt them beyond their ability to resist. I believed that if this particular nurse had progressed any further in her efforts to take care of my surgical preparation, I would have had to write to Salt Lake City and tell them that I no longer believed in that particular tenet of faith.

Finally, the nurse grabbed hold of a hypodermic needle rather than the razor. She lifted it and squirted a drop or two out of the end of the needle before inserting it deeply and directly into my right buttock. After removing the needle, she set the hypodermic down on the cart, smiled at me, and then wished me good luck. With that, she turned and exited my room. It turned out that God was smarter than I thought. He wasn't going to tempt me beyond my will to resist and had saved me from a very embarrassing situation.

After a male orderly took care of the shaving duties, I was placed on a gurney and rolled off toward surgery. I remember, as if it were yesterday, the feeling I got as I was rolled down the hallway toward an elevator at the end of the hall. One orderly was at the foot of my gurney, and another was at the head. They, along with myself, were the only ones in the hallway. Nevertheless, I felt the distinct presence of some one else, though I saw no one. At once, I realized that my brief supplication to God in Lumphoon had been answered. A guardian angel, as it were, had been with me from the moment of that prayer all the way up to my being rolled into surgery. He had comforted me and protected me. As afraid as I was at the time of my prayer, I had not given it another nervous thought since leaving Lumphoon. I had gone tracting, participated in a street meeting, gone to church, and even played basketball, and I had had no problems. God had not only heard my prayer, He had answered it.

The surgery went smoothly, at least that is what I was told, and my recovery was uneventful and complete. However, as a part of the recovery, I had to spend two weeks in the mission home. Now it is not that President and Sister Morris were not great hosts, nor was it that their four sons were any more trouble than any other four sons might be to a house guest. Rather, what bothered me was that I was spending two weeks away from what had become a way of life for me. I read every Archie comic in the house, along with some other less-noteworthy titles. I also caught up on all the letters I owed to people, and after a couple of days, began playing ping-pong with the boys. Almost immediately, one son, Todd, observed that once my body became planted in a particular spot behind the table, it was there to stay, and I could only play balls hit within arm's reach. While I do have long arms, they aren't long enough to extend to the outer edges of the table. Todd took full advantage. Because Todd was as mean as I was in extracting victories from helpless victims under any circumstances, I took great pleasure in routinely knocking him off later on in my recovery, when my mobility began to return. Once I began playing football in the yard with Todd, Layne, Collin, Rhen, and the gardener, it became clear I was ready to return to Lumphoon and the job of being a missionary.

XI

SMALL TOWN FUN

Returning to Lumphoon was like going home. Elder Kirby picked me up at the train station along with Elder Thayne, who hailed from Syracuse, Utah. Strangely, I was a little bit surprised at my irritation at having been replaced in Lumphoon by Elder Thayne. He was a good guy and all, but it was as if he had sat in my chair, ate my porridge, and slept in my bed. It turned out that in a very short time, I had become very attached to Lumphoon.

Elder Thayne stayed with Elder Kirby and me that first day back and we all tracted together. Elder Thayne actually was a rather enjoyable companion for a day, but I was truly relieved to take him to the train station for his ride back to his own district. As is typical of the bureaucratic process in Thailand, the ticket agent would only give Elder Thayne a sitting car space, saying that no sleeping cars were available. I later learned that we were correct when we assumed that once Elder Thayne got on the train, he would be able to pay a little extra money to one of the conductors who would find an available sleeper car.

In no time at all, I was back in the routine of things, with the lone exception that I was grounded from riding a bicycle for a couple of weeks. Hence, tracting became more of a labor of love than it had been in the past. By the end of a day, it seemed we had covered several miles, and we probably had. As I mentioned earlier, tracting in the States was a horrible bore and, quite often, became quite destructive of one's self image; that was not the case in Thailand. Tracting provided a wealth of opportunities to meet new people and expose our ideas to those who had never considered a Christian way of life.

Between tracting and teaching English at a local school and at the hospital, Elder Kirby and I were able to meet a small group of individuals with whom we scheduled weekly appointments to teach the Mormon dogma.

Piichion had become one of our regular appointments. He was very gregarious, and by his genuine smile, I knew that he truly enjoyed our meetings. Unfortunately for the church, Piichion was always more interested in our American background than in our religious lessons. Nevertheless, his willingness to spend countless hours with us did afford me the opportunity to practice my missionary lessons and sharpen my language skills. It just wasn't very likely that Piichion was ever going to become a member of the church, though we never completely gave up on him.

Our contacts ranged from Piichion all the way to Phatcharaphon (*PUTT-chah-rah-pahn*), who almost always appeared at our meetings in her white nurse's uniform. She was quietly proud to be a nurse. She was readily accepting of all those around her, and had more than an engaging smile. She was always a pleasure to be around. Her large brown eyes seemed always to evidence a warm embracing of everything we told her. She truly seemed hungry for the ideas and concepts we provided her. It became a highlight of every week to have Phatcharaphon come to us for her lessons.

I could not wait to learn my Thai vocabulary words during the week so that I could continue teaching Phatcharaphon new concepts about Jesus Christ and the Mormon Church. For when I would teach, the satisfaction to me was being able to look into her eyes and see how warmly she embraced and accepted the simple ideas that God was her Father and that He loved and cared for her, so much so, that He gave His Only Begotten Son, Jesus Christ, as a sacrifice for all of our sins. Never have I seen this message bring so much peace and joy to anyone. Phatcharaphon, like Brother Mani in Thonburi, will live brightly in my mind and heart for as long as I breathe on this earth.

In addition to Piichion and Phatcharaphon, we had various other contacts whose interests would run hot and cold. Khamnung *(CUM nung)* was a brother-in-law to my LTM teacher, Elder Mongkon. At first, Khamnung was willing to listen to our message only as a favor to Mongkon, who seemed quietly desperate for us to be successful in not only teaching Khamnung but also converting him to the church. While I enjoyed Khamnung's company and my visits with him, I could tell that he did not have any present interest in abandoning his heritage in favor of the "liberal" Western religion of his brother-in-law.

Another consistent appointment was with a very tiny thirteen-year-old girl named Aat *(At)*. Aat was a typical young teenager, if ever I had seen one. She had short bobbed black hair, inquisitive brown eyes, and a mood that I could swear was swinging both up and down at the same time. Though we never baptized her, Aat became our Sunday school chorister. That is not to say that she always had a congregation to lead, unless you were to consider Elder Kirby and me a congregation.

More often than not, we did have visitors drop by to experience our Sunday Christian meetings. Piichion, Khamnung, Phatcharaphon, and Aat, along with various other infrequent visitors, would come and listen to my Sunday school lessons. Initially, I often wondered if they could understand anything I was saying. However, as the weeks rolled on in Lumphoon, I became more and more confident and more and more capable. I would see fewer and fewer screwed-up faces peering at me as if I were speaking a language from another planet. More and more, people would simply talk to me about the content of our discussion. Language was finally becoming something of a non-issue for me in Thailand.

I had now been in Thailand for some six months and continued to work as a junior companion. Such status, depending upon who your senior companion was, could be equated with the untouchable class in India. As a junior companion, you had no ultimate say in anything you did. I never found such status to be appealing and, in fact, have never been very good at simply taking directions. Fortunately for me, my first two senior companions, Elders Peckham and Kirby, were quite laid back, and therefore, leader-friendly.

My first chance to actually be in charge of anything occurred when Elder Kirby's visa expired. Consequently, he had to make the obligatory trip to Bangkok, where he met with the other missionaries who came with him to Thailand, and then rode the "blue pig" (a large blue Dodge van owned by the mission) to Aranyaprathet (*Ah-run-yah-brah-TADE*), a small town just across the Cambodian border. All missionaries had to take their turns renewing their visas in Cambodia at two-and-a-half month intervals during my days in

Thailand. In fact, one missionary was assigned the full-time job of simply keeping track of all the missionaries' visitor's visas, renewing them as long as possible, and then rounding up those whose visas were about to expire and carting them off to Cambodia for renewal. It was not a pleasant job for the missionary assigned as the visa secretary, nor was it directly productive in terms of missionary work. On the other hand, I always had a great time getting together with all my old missionary buddies from the LTM every two-and-a-half months to spend a day catching up on all the latest mission tales.

Tracting stories abounded since missionaries spent a substantial amount of their time going from door to door, seeking ears interested in hearing about the church. Occasionally, adults would send children to answer the door with instructions to say that no one else was home. Oftentimes you could hear the parents of those children giving the instructions. After tiring of such cowardice, a missionary on one occasion proceeded to tell the child in a loud voice that it was too bad there was no adult at home, as he was a representative of the Coca-Cola Company, and he was there to announce to the owner of the home that he or she had just won ten thousand *baht*. Now he would have to seek a new winner elsewhere. He rehearsed to us with joy, the satisfaction he got when the child's parents suddenly appeared out of the back of the house, only to be told that the offer had to be withdrawn since he had been told by the child that no one was at home.

Other mission tales included topics as divergent as drawing targets on elders' arms so that Sister Morris would know where to inject gamma globulin shots, to stories of burglaries at the missionaries' homes, to bus accidents in Bangkok, and to rumors as to who was going to be transferred where, next.

In any event, Elder Kirby and I traveled to Chiang Mai, where he boarded a train to Bangkok and I was able to partner up with Elder Humphries. Elder Humphries was a person the likes of whom I had never really experienced up close before. He had been born and raised in Enterprise, Utah, a town in the southwestern part of that state. Enterprise was so small that on the Fourth of July each year, the entire town could gather on the front lawn of the church and hold foot races to determine who the fastest kids in town were. His southern Utah drawl was unmistakable and became absolutely comical when mixed with Thai. Elder Humphries was very bright, but was never the greatest at losing his Southern Utah drawl when speaking Thai, but his heart was as big as a southern Utah cattle ranch and the Thai people loved him for it.

I remember experiencing his farewell from Chiang Mai a few months after buddying up with him for the three days that Elder Kirby was renewing his visa. It must be remembered that at the time, the Chiang Mai branch of the church had no more than twenty members. But when Elder Humphries left, they were all with him at the train station crying and waving good-bye to their most cherished and prized American missionary friend. The experience confirmed to me that there was no real language barrier that would ultimately preclude me from touching the heart of anyone in Thailand, so long as I was anywhere near as kindhearted as Elder Humphries. Easier said than done.

A couple of weeks after Elder Kirby returned from his dash to Cambodia, we received a somewhat unexpected message from President Morris. He had read Elder Kirby's request for permission to travel with Piichion to the Thai-Burmese border to take in the sights and spend time with one of our contacts. President Morris expressed envy at the opportunity for the experience, cautioned us to be careful, told us to remember who we were, and then said to have a great experience. I was thrilled, and Elder Kirby was somewhat dumbstruck. Regardless, we immediately went to Piichion and told him we would like to go with him on his next trip to work.

Piichion was a light-hearted fellow who was always quick with a smile. But upon hearing that his two American novelties would be accompanying him on his next work trip, a smile washed over Piichion that I thought might well break his face. Within two days, we were off in the Thai equivalent of a "big-rig" truck, something they called a ten wheeler. In the United States, a big rig was considered decorated if it had a metallic outline of a reclining female on each mud flap. Thai truckers would have scoffed at such minimalist efforts. Our ten-wheeler was decked out with at least fifty colored running lights all around, with a bright blue cab and more chrome figurines than the Teamsters could imagine. And this was all on one truck. Elder Kirby and I traveled in the cab with Piichion for the better part of a day into the heart of the Golden Triangle.

We arrived at what was to be our home for the next two days just before dusk. This village was some seventy-five miles northwest of Chiang Mai. There was no water, gas, or electricity, and for that matter, there was no plaster or concrete either. I had never been so far away from anything civilized in my life. Piichion pulled up to a small thatch roofed, one-room hut that was no more than six-and-a-half feet in total height. Piichion bragged that this hut was his own creation and was one of the only huts in the village with a wooden floor. I thought about debating Piichion as to whether or not the floor of the hut was really wooden, but decided to let him revel in his fantasy.

The people of the village were quite different from any Thais whom I had seen before. In fact, Piichion explained that other than living within Thai sovereign territory, these people were not Thai at all. They had their own language and their own semi-nomadic culture. They had come to rely on the opium trade for their existence, which at the time was quite lucrative. Unfortunately for the hill tribesmen, protection money was exacted from them by both Thai and Burmese officials, although the payoffs never did seem to totally protect them from periodic raids by communist insurgents.

I was at or near the end of the world. The only interruption in the jungle foliage was where the hill tribesmen had carved out poppy fields. Connecting the few permanent villages in the area was a dirt road that would wash out every rainy season. Piichion's job was to keep the road open as far as possible, which meant that in the morning we would be traveling even closer to the Burmese border to observe Piichion in his work.

It seems that government work never can get finished and is, therefore, always around. I guess no matter where you go in the world, it is the way of things. For example, I remember a judge in Southern California before whom I recently appeared to defend an employer in a wrongful termination case. He was quite laid back and relaxed, and admonished us before the trial began to approach things the same way. He had counted up the number of cases in his charge and realized that no matter how hard he worked, he would be no closer to completing his job at retirement than if he were to simply relax and avoid the stress of trying to catch up, where catching up was not part of the plan anyway.

At the time of the admonition by the judge, I remember thinking that many a housewife probably feels the same way about her thankless and endless job.

Apparently, Piichion had the same attitude. With his American friends in tow, he spent no more than two hours on his bulldozer.

Granted, it did seem to be quite a productive two hours. There was a stretch of road approximately one hundred fifty yards in length that had been completely washed away. Within the two hours, Piichion had graded a new path, making the road passable again. While the road was certainly not perfect, it was passable and Piichion explained that no matter what he did, the next rain storm would create just as much work for him again. With that, Piichion turned off the Caterpillar and left it standing by the side of his newly refurbished road and then said, "Let's go."

Off into the jungle, he bolted, as he explained with pride the unique characteristics and history of the hills we were exploring. Admittedly, I could only tell of his pride by the tone of his voice. He was so far out in front of me and speaking so quickly that, even when I could hear him, I could barely make out what he was saying. Periodically, he would turn around to make sure we were still following him, the corners of his smile virtually touching the lobes of his ears. It was great fun to see the child-like joy that Piichion displayed that day.

After clamoring over a few small but steep hills, we found ourselves on the side of a veritable mountain (by comparison), approaching a small twenty-by-thirty-foot hut. A well had been dug to provide water, and an outhouse provided almost all the amenities of home. A grizzled old Thai poked his head out of the hut and, upon seeing Piichion, set his gun down by the side of the door, came out, and greeted Piichion warmly. After Piichion explained who we were, we were also welcomed. While Piichion and his old friend became reacquainted, several teenage boys assembled around us. They were all carrying long barreled rifles, and it turned out that they would be taking us on a hike.

It was not too long after my hernia surgery, and so I felt that we had already been on a hike. But the prospect of seeing more of this wilderness was too much to resist, and we were off. Shortly, we were walking through rather deeply forested areas. Hanging from the trees were vines only Tarzan could fully appreciate.

One of the teenagers handed me his long-barreled rifle and invited me to shoot at a bird that was off in the distance. First of all, it took me a long time to figure out that he was inviting me to shoot his gun, as he was not speaking Thai; and even if he was, my religiously based vocabulary had not included terms that would describe the firing of a weapon. Further, I was always conscious of the fact that I was a Mormon missionary who was supposed to be spreading a gospel of love. Somehow, shooting a bird did not seem to correspond with that mandate.

Regardless and ultimately, I did take the gun as I sat on a log to help prop up the long barrel of the gun, and I looked for my prey. There was no scope on the gun, nor were there even cross-hairs to help aim. How these fellows could ever hit anything with this gun was beyond me, but I was actually becoming excited to give it a try. As best I could, I sighted in the bird off the top edge of the barrel and tried to squeeze (rather than pull) the trigger. Much to my surprise, nothing happened, at least for a second or two. As I loosened my grip on the rifle, preparing to hand it back to my guide, I heard a sudden blast and felt an immediate and sharp pain to my right shoulder as I went vaulting backwards over the back of a log, completely unaware of what had happened.

As I lay on my back on the ground behind the log, the long-barreled rifle still in my hands, I looked up and saw that everyone but Elder Kirby was laughing. They were having a wonderful time. Elder Kirby had wondered if I had broken my shoulder. It turned out that the long barreled rifle was a flintlock type of gun, and, therefore, did not fire immediately upon having the trigger squeezed. The rifle had worked just fine. I had just forgotten that hiking back into the hill country had transported us back to American Revolutionary War times in terms of weaponry.

As the end of the day approached, it was time for a bath. I was handed a bolt of red-and-white-checked cloth and was led to a stream, where a stalk of bamboo had been split in half to channel water for drinking and bathing purposes. One end of the stalk was placed into the stream, with the other end was simply allowed to hang out about two feet above the stream, approximately five feet downstream. Our guides each took a turn in the stream and then invited Elder Kirby and me to join them.

Elder Kirby steadfastly declined the offer, following the admonition from the church that missionaries should avoid any and all bodies of water (I guess with the lone exception of that water which would come from a shower nozzle or faucet in a sink). Such a belief comes from the notion that Satan has control of the waters and would particularly like to bring about his evil doings by drowning Mormon missionaries.

I looked down at the stream, which was no more than a foot deep, and decided that I would risk it. I joined the guides in frolicking mostly, and cleaning secondarily. The stream was cold, but quite refreshing. The look of my long, skinny, and pasty-white body provided our guides with more amusement and laughter. Regardless, I was clean and refreshed and none-the-worse for the attention.

When you hike into an area, it should be remembered that you must also hike out. The late afternoon was therefore spent hiking back to Piichion's friend's hut and then clamoring over the hills to his truck, where we climbed in and rode back to the village.

Our trip to the hill tribes was a great success. Elder Kirby and I saw things that we had not seen before, and I anticipate I will never see again. The jungles, the waterfalls, and the people all made for great memories. I learned that people could be happy in all kinds of circumstances. Piichion became a fast and close friend, one who would not distrust Americans in the future and one who might actually someday embrace the Christian way of life. And for Piichion, he became some thing of a celebrity in those hills: he had friends all the way from America.

Upon returning to Lumphoon, we received written notification that Elder Kirby had been transferred to Lumphang *(Lum-PANG)*. Lumphang was only an hour or so south of Lumphoon, but it was far enough away that I would not see much of Elder Kirby again. We traveled to the furniture maker to make sure he was completing the podium and sacrament table for our church and then packed Elder Kirby up for his move. The upside to this news was that my new companion was to be Elder Morgan Warner, the missionary who gave me my first glimpses of Bangkok on my first day in the country. I had enjoyed his company then and was anxious to spend time with him now.

XII

WORD OF WISDOM

Just before Elder Kirby's departure, the nurses and doctors at the hospital in Lumphoon, knowing I had recently undergone a hernia operation in Bangkok, were anxious to show me what the operation looked like. So after our weekly English lesson was completed with the nurses at the hospital, Elder Kirby and I donned our gowns, gloves, and masks and went into the operating room at the hospital to watch a hernia repair procedure. The surgeon was thrilled to have American visitors in the operating room and spent more time explaining what he was doing than actually doing what he was explaining.

The patient's lower abdomen had been swabbed with a terribly ugly orange disinfectant. The surgeon took hold of his scalpel and, without so much as a moment's hesitation, gently pressed the sharp edge of the scalpel to the patient's skin. For only an instant, the blade indented the skin before smoothly parting several layers of the epidermis down into the fatty tissue. The doctor then continued by making about a four-inch incision in the patient's lower abdomen.

For me, this was the worst part of the operation to watch. Only three or four weeks before, the same thing had happened to me, except that it was bilateral. I do not mind saying that I got pretty queasy and started to feel rather weak in the knees. Thankfully, the surgeon began explaining the procedure to me in detail, which took my mind off of the incision. The patient had what was called a strangulated hernia. This sounded quite serious to me, but, in fact, I had no idea what a strangulated hernia was. I was soon to find out. The doctor continued cutting through layers of fat and tissue until he actually could reach down into the bowels of this poor guy.

The surgeon then began pulling lengths of intestine out of the patient's abdomen and laying them upon his chest. I then began to feel queazy all over again as the nurse took the exposed lengths of intestine into her hands and wrapped them in a warm towel. She then began to slowly massage the intestine as if she was preparing an athlete for some type of sporting event.

I am sure that the surgeon was reading my total ignorance of the entire situation on my face at this point. He completely stopped working and instructed the nurse to show me the dark spots on that portion of the intestine that she was holding in her hands. He explained that the length of intestine the nurse was massaging had been oxygen-starved for a period of time, and the nurse was trying to work blood back into that portion of the intestine. If the intestine got its color back, then everything was fine. If not, then he would have to cut out those portions of the intestine that had been completely strangulated.

This portion of the surgeon's explanation was filled with so many new Thai vocabulary words that I had to speculate as to various portions of the lesson. Besides, my own loins were suffering a great deal of sympathy pain at this point, and I was becoming quite anxious for the surgeon to stop explaining things to me and continue with his work on this poor patient. Thankfully for the patient and for me, the intestine seemed to respond well to the nurse's towel work. Ultimately, the patient's intestine was flopped back into his abdominal cavity and the doctor began sewing the patient back up.

I was amazed that in inserting the intestine back into the abdominal cavity, there seemed to be no particular concern over just how the intestine was reinserted. Instead, it was just kind of shoved back in. When I asked the surgeon about this, he laughed and simply explained that everything seems to arrange itself okay on its own. My first thought was that I was glad I was not that patient. Almost immediately, however, I remembered that just a short three or four weeks earlier I had been that patient. I could only hope that my innards were smart enough to finally come to rest right where they belonged.

Typically, when moves are announced, the elders are given two to three days to pack up and say good-bye. The packing up is easy, the saying good-bye is not. Elder Kirby and I had become fast friends with several people in Lumphoon and it was time for him to say good-bye to them. The English class we had been teaching at the hospital arranged for a luncheon, which garnered us a follow-up invitation to attend a party at the hospital the next night, welcoming the incoming director.

Since the nurses made the arrangements for the party, they took great care to seat us at the table with the new director. The director's mother was the hostess, and was gracious almost to the point of embarrassing us, as we were fussed over more than her own son, the new director.

I also remember that this woman was an avid betel nut chewer with all the disgusting evidences of the habit very visible. My minimal experience with chewing tobacco in the United States was bad enough, but betel nut turned out to be far worse. The chewer doesn't just drool on himself or herself as a tobacco chewer might do, but because of its slightly narcotic effect, the imbiber also becomes lethargic and quite sloppy. The betel nut juice is red, and over time, creates a disgusting red stain down each side of a chewer's mouth, just as you would imagine the stains of a gutter that passes sewage and other filth along its way. I am not really sure that there is a more disgusting habit in the world than chewing betel nut. In any event, the sight of this woman serving us dinner was quite repulsive, and I constantly worried about whether or not she was going to drool on my food. The same concern did not seem to affect any of the other participants at the dinner. I guess there are some things that just don't bother you, if that's what you grow up with.

Elder Kirby and I had met several very good people in Lumphoon during our three months together, and it was now time to say good-bye to the best of all of them: Phatcharaphon. We spent about two hours with Phatcharaphon trading postage stamps and hearing her description of Lumphang. Of all the people we were teaching, Elder Kirby made me promise not to give up on Phatcharaphon.

That Sunday was the second week in a row that we had five adults attending church services. For us, five adults in one meeting felt like a standing-room-only event. Our Sunday School lesson that week began with a discussion of Adam's transgression and the resulting fall of man. It quickly progressed through the Atonement of Jesus Christ and on into the hopes and fears of what was to lie ahead for all of us in the next life. In a one-hour period, we had covered several topics, any one of which, considered alone, has created great controversies in the Christian world for two thousand years. Nevertheless, everyone present seemed extremely interested in these various Christian concepts that, to the Thai people, were all brand new.

After church and a brief meeting with Aat, to whom we taught an additional part of the discussions, Elder Kirby and I boarded the bus and traveled to Chiang Mai for the wedding of the branch president there. It was a traditional Chinese wedding that included the drinking of wine, a highly symbolic gesture in the Chinese wedding ceremony. President Suchad *(Soo-CHAHD)* was a good church member and had agonized over whether or not he should drink the ceremonial wine. He finally decided to go along with the tradition, to the extent that he would at least press the cup of wine to his lips. The gesture seemed hypocritical to me and, therefore, extremely distasteful. I had been taught that either you believed you were not supposed to drink alcohol or you didn't. There was no middle ground. But is there?

Section 89 of the church's *Doctrine and Covenants* teaches that "strong drinks are not for the belly." From that, the Mormon Church has developed an absolute position on alcohol, to wit, that the ingestion of any alcoholic beverage constitutes sin. In fact, such a practice will keep one from being able to worship in the temple.

Witnessing this Chinese wedding ceremony, and President Suchad's deception in pretending to drink the ceremonial wine, gave me great pause to reflect on my own beliefs about Section 89 of the *Doctrine and Covenants,* or the "Word of Wisdom[10]." On the one hand, the church had developed an absolute position that Section 89 categorically precluded the consumption of alcohol, tea, and coffee. On the other hand, the language of the section is more advisory than absolute.

Some in the church at various times have even gone so far as to say that "hot drinks," specifically mentioned in Section 89 of the *Doctrine and Covenants,* included all caffeinated drinks and that therefore Coca-Cola was also taboo. For myself, I had to conclude that such manipulation of the actual revelatory word was well beyond anything that God had ever intended. I note from firsthand experience that Coca-Cola is not a "hot drink." Besides, if Coca-Cola is taboo because it is caffeinated, why then is not chocolate also declared to be out of bounds as a "hot drink" due to its caffeine content?

It seemed to me that a more practical interpretation of Section 89 was to simply read the words as recorded and try to live them. If we did, we would be blessed so as to be able to "run and not be weary, and walk and not faint." After all, that is the promise given to those who comply with the admonition of the Word of Wisdom.

As it is, though, so long as you don't smoke or drink alcohol, coffee, or tea, members are declared to be followers of the Word of Wisdom and are invited to participate in the temple ceremonies. It does not really matter what other horrible things you might do to your body, as is evidenced by the number of people attending the temple who would no doubt benefit from some time at a gym instead.

This issue of the Word of Wisdom was a gnarly one for me and not one to be taken lightly. Was the drinking of a Coca-Cola a violation of the Word of Wisdom, or was it not? One day, after riding a great distance to an investigator's home and then traveling with that investigator to a small restaurant to eat, I was advised that I was violating the Word of Wisdom by drinking a Coca-Cola. I asked our Thai friend, "Who told you that drinking Coca-Cola was a violation of the Word of Wisdom?"

"When I was in Bangkok, one of the missionaries there told me that drinking Coca-Cola was a violation of the Word of Wisdom and that good Mormons could not drink such a beverage," he replied.

I was caught short for want of an appropriate reply. Should I respond by saying that the missionary who so informed him was just some fanatic nut who was no different from the Pharisees at the time of Christ who could understand only rules and not the spirit of the law? Or should I explain to him my conclusions about the subtleties of the Word of Wisdom as I saw them and the fact that it was a challenge to maintain your body as a healthy tabernacle for your spirit? Or was there some other more appropriate explanation in between?

I worried that if I actually gave this good Thai fellow my real opinion on the matter, other missionaries present would chastise me for teaching a doctrine that was out of harmony with the common message of the day from the General Authorities. Besides, I wasn't too sure that my Thai was good enough to actually articulate the more subtle nuances of my position. I therefore passed the *phat Thai (putt tai)* and invited my good Thai friend to eat up.

XIII

THE TOE

Elder Warner came to Lumphoon with a recently received care package from home, filled with cookies and candies that all probably fall outside of the parameters of the intent of the Word of Wisdom. Still, we ate every crumb.

On our first full day together, Elder Warner and I taught English at the hospital, which was always great fun. Then we tracted for a couple hours, which was also enjoyable because we were either able to teach somebody about the gospel or just enjoy the sights. In the evening, I was able to introduce Elder Warner to Phatcharaphon. As we had gotten to know Phatcharaphon, we began to refer to her as Sister Phatcharaphon. This reference is an indication that she was coming into the church family, even though she had not yet committed to baptism. Sister Phatcharaphon was the first golden contact[11] I had ever met and taught.

In fact, I only met one other golden contact that I was aware of in my whole mission. By this time, we were teaching her at least one time per week. She always had lots of questions about what we were teaching her, which meant that she was actually paying attention to what was said rather than just having a good time with a couple of weird Americans. Elder Warner and I sat down after teaching Sister Phatcharaphon and mapped out a strategy for trying to teach her all that she needed to know to become a member of the Mormon Church.

Elder Warner was my third senior companion, and the first one who wasn't engaged, or at least close to it. Consequently, his moods seemed to be much more constant than Elders Peckham or Kirby, and did not vacillate up and down based upon whether or not he received the much anticipated mail from a girlfriend.

That did not mean the subject of girls never came up during our time together. In fact, within a week of Elder Warner coming to Lumphoon, females became an object of a brief but pointed discussion. Elder Warner and I were riding our bikes on the narrow ridge dividing two rice paddies. This ridge was no more than twelve inches in width, and if you rode off of one side or the other, then you would find your self mid-calf deep in a rice paddy. Hence, it was essential to pay close attention to the ride.

As we rode along, with me traveling in front of Elder Warner, a Thai approached us on foot. The closer we got to this person, the more I could see. She was very attractive and was wearing a very, very sheer blouse with nothing on underneath it. Now, I was a twenty-year-old boy who had taken a vow of celibacy and more for two years. I intended to keep my vows, but that did not mean I had become blind. We carefully passed by this young lady and peddled on, but I could not help but look back at what I considered to be something of a vision at the time.

My senior companion patiently indulged my whim, and, in fact, briefly joined me. However, Elder Warner was my senior companion for a good reason. His glance was more of a glance and my stare was more of a stare, which meant that Elder Warner was able to return his eyes to the path we were traveling, as opposed to staring back at the path we had traveled.

"Look out!" yelled Elder Warner.

I turned my head to see what was before me, only to find that I was no more than a foot or two from a large tree that loomed ahead. I slammed on my foot brake and cranked the wheel to avoid the tree, which I did. Unfortunately, I did not avoid the rice paddy or the embarrassment, as I was standing calf-deep in the rice paddy.

Elder Warner asked, "Was the view worth it?" I could only respond, "Let me think about it." But inside, I had to admit to myself that it was.

Oddly enough, at about the same time, we were attempting to advertise our evening English class to recruit additional students to come to our home. As a result of our efforts, this same young woman appeared in our English class about a week later. I asked Elder Warner to teach the English class that evening and retired to the back of the room, where I read scriptures during the class time. I did not believe it would be a good idea for me to be anywhere near the cause of my earlier mental diversion.

Elder Warner and I enjoyed tracting and were meeting lots of people I had not seen before, even though I thought that Elder Kirby and I had just about tracted out the entire city. Lumphoon was a small town, but I had not yet tired of it.

Oftentimes, late in the afternoon, I would go out to the vacant lot next door to our home and play *ta graw* (*dah grah*) with the neighborhood kids. *Ta graw* is a game played with a ball made of strips of bamboo-like material woven into a round ball. The game is similar to volleyball, except that you cannot use your hands or arms except for the back of your arm from the elbow to the shoulder. Otherwise, you can use any other part of your body. Instead of a net, the neighborhood kids used a rope at a height of approximately five feet. That was perfect for me, a six-footer. If the *ta graw* ball came low over the rope, I could slam dunk it back across the rope with my head. The only drawback was that I would occasionally get thumped in the head by a high-kicking opponent. All in all, it was great fun.

Strangely, playing *ta graw* with the neighborhood kids turned out to be something akin to a sideshow. We began attracting older teenagers, and then adults, who would simply stand around and chat as they watched. Slowly, we got to know all of our neighbors without making too much of a spectacle of ourselves. (Well, there had been one exception to the non-spectacle-type performance back with Elder Kirby. He tried to recover a ball headed out-of-bounds once and fell into some barbed wire. I guess the five to ten minutes it took to extricate him from the barbed wire would constitute something of a spectacle.)

Elder Warner and I continued teaching all who would listen to us in Lumphoon. We would lose some investigators and gain others along the way, our numbers remaining basically constant. The discouraging part was that we could not seem to move anyone far enough along to get them committed to baptism. Piichion and Khumnung were very consistent in participating in the missionary discussions. On the other hand, it did not feel that they were moving very far, very fast down the road toward baptism. Sisters Phatcharaphon and Aat did seem to be providing us with some degree of hope until Sister Phatcharaphon announced that she was taking a nursing position in Bangkok, which was providing her with a promotion and an increase in pay. Her announcement was very hard to take, not only because we were getting close to actually having a baptism in Lumphoon that would now not occur, but also because I would be losing a very good friend.

It had become time for my second trip to Cambodia to renew my visa and I, therefore, traveled to Chiang Mai and boarded the sleeper train to Bangkok. On the way south, Elder Welling boarded the train in Lumphang and we had a great mini-reunion on the ride. I specifically recall the topic of discussion that night as being the next step in our lives after our missions were completed. Typically, a young man in the Mormon Church is baptized at eight, ordained to the Aaronic Priesthood[12] and set apart as a deacon[12] at twelve, promoted to teacher[12] at fourteen, and then again, promoted to priest[2] at age sixteen. At age nineteen, he is expected to serve a mission after taking on the mantle of the Melchizedek Priesthood[3] as an elder[1]. At the same time, he is asked to take out his endowment at the temple, where he commits his life to the temple covenants.

Following the mission experience, he is expected to return home, seek out a wife, and marry. Hence, we talked about the next step: marriage. It just seemed to be that getting married was a given as the next step in a young man's church life after his mission, but no missionary wanted to be the first in his group to be married.

We attempted to rank our group of twelve missionaries in terms of who would be married first, second, third, and so on down the line. We believed that Elder Judkins, as a real ladies' man, would go first and that Elder Humphries, who seemed quite content to worry about how the next hay season would go, would be last. The rest of us ranged somewhere in between. I only remember that Elder Montgomery was slated as the number two man and that I would probably go fifth. Was there any rhyme or reason to any of this? Probably not. But realizing that marriage was the next duty for all young Mormon men following their missions, it certainly was a topic of consideration and discussion.

As was always the case, the drive to Cambodia was hot and tiring, and yet extremely enjoyable as the twelve of us who had come to Thailand together had a chance to become reacquainted. The biggest news of this particular trip was that Elder Pace's girlfriend, who we all had supposed would become his wife, wrote to tell him she was getting married. We had presumed that his position with his girlfriend was quite solid, but the rankings that we had just constructed coming from Lumphoon would clearly have to be reconsidered in light of this news, and Elder Pace needed time to adjust.

Upon returning to Lumphoon, we discovered that a light had been left on in the bathroom upstairs while we were gone. Unfortunately, the light served as a rallying point for every bug and spider in Lumphoon. I thought the house was going to be lifted off its shaky foundation and carried away by the multitude. It was my one chance to play Rambo, and I believe that Sylvester Stallone would have been proud of me. I did the only thing I could. I mounted my tank-like two-wheeler and peddled off to the one and only supermarket (okay, it was more like an AM/PM mini-mart) in Lumphoon. There I purchased the last two cans of Raid on the shelf, and then returned home outfitted for battle. Two cans of Raid later, I had done away with almost as many bugs, spiders, and ants as *Rambo* has killed off enemy combatants and other bad guys in his various adventures around the world. Unfortunately, I had also inhaled enough of the Raid to choke an ox. The battle probably cost me five years off the end of my life.

Bugs weren't the only critters to be concerned about in Lumphoon. Close to the house was a large open field filled with marsh-like tall grass that we rode by almost every night, returning home from our various excursions. One evening, when returning home from a teaching appointment, I was leisurely peddling by the field when out from amongst the blades of tall grass leapt a three-foot-long, bright green snake. It missed me, but grazed my back tire and then retreated back into the protective grass. I don't mind saying that I was scared to death. That snake was out to get me, and I could not help but wonder if he had heard about my assault on bugdom a few days earlier. At my next English class at the hospital, I was told by one of the doctors that such bright green snakes were extremely venomous. From that date forward, I always traversed that part of the road home as rapidly as possible, and on the opposite side of the street.

Over time, Elder Warner and I turned that stretch of road into a speedway, and we would race each other home nightly. On one such occasion, Elder Warner had gained the inside lane on me, which put him on the opposite side of the road from the grass. Lining that other side of the road were small wooden houses that had been built up off the ground by about five steps. On this particular evening, a small girl was riding her little bike out into the street at the time Elder Warner made his sweeping inside turn to the left. His collision with the little girl was at full speed, and he went toppling head over heels over the handlebars. Much worse, the little girl fell with her bicycle sailing over her head. Elder Warner and the little girl came to rest some distance apart and laid rather still for an uncomfortable period of time. Finally, the little girl began to sob quietly, and Elder Warner slowly rose to his feet, shook himself off, and walked over to the little girl to see how she was.

It seemed that whenever American missionaries were involved in anything that went on in Thailand, a crowd was the natural result, and this event was no exception. A group of fifteen to twenty people gathered around. A young chubby Chinese boy about ten-years-old was inspecting the little girl and her bike for some time when he yelled out, "Look, her toe isn't there!" pointing to her left foot. "It's over there!" pointing then to the sprocket of the little girl's bicycle.

Sure enough, the accident had severed the girl's little toe from her little foot. The realization of this fact by the little girl immediately changed her sobs to shrieks of horror. Elder Warner became quite pale and paralyzed with grief and panic himself.

I summoned a three-wheeled bicycle taxi and lifted the girl into the seat, instructing the driver to take her directly to the hospital. As the driver mounted his three-wheel taxi bike, the observant Chinese boy ran over to the little girl's bike, pulled the little toe from the bicycle sprocket, and threw it on the floor of the three-wheeled bicycle taxi where the little girl was seated. Off they went to the hospital, and after Elder Warner had a moment or two to recover his senses, we also headed off to the hospital.

The doctors did not even try to reattach the little toe, but simply stitched up the foot after disinfecting it, and then, after bandaging it, placed a white sock on her foot, instructing her to keep the white sock as clean as possible for the next week.

For that next week, Elder Warner was not very good at being a proselyting missionary. He could not get his mind off what had happened. We visited the little girl every day and reminded her constantly to keep her sock clean. At the end of the week, Elder Warner gave the little girl and her family two hundred *baht*, which is the equivalent of approximately ten dollars, to cover the little girl's medical expenses. Her parents thanked us and the traumatic event was concluded. (Parenthetically, that certainly would not be the end of the incident if it had happened in the United States, as there would have followed the obligatory legal action to recover damages for not only medical expenses, but also for pain and suffering and anything else that could be dreamed up, such as loss of visual symmetry of the feet).

A few days of good, hard, fruitless tracting followed the incident, and things slowly returned to normal for Elder Warner. It was about this time that I received a very welcomed care package from home. My mother had sent me a one-pound bag of M&M's and a large box of Sugar Smacks cereal. My favorites. If I could be guaranteed a continuing stream of M&M's and Sugar Smacks, I could easily see staying in the mission field for the rest of my life. Elder Warner and I took care of the M&M's in short order.

The Sugar Smacks posed another problem. They had been completely infested by ants, and I just couldn't figure out how to get those ants to leave me and my Sugar Smacks alone. It did ultimately dawn on me that I could probably float the ants away with milk, and in pursuing my theory went ahead and poured myself a bowl of the wondrous cereal. Sure enough, the ants, or at least most of them, floated to the top, and I simply scooped off the majority of those little buggers and then proceeded to enjoy my cereal without further interruption. I do not believe I would repeat this process again, but those were desperate times, and I hadn't seen a Sugar Smack in almost a year.

XIV

WATER FESTIVAL

Khumnung was still willing to listen to our lessons and, while I was never too hopeful that he would actually join the church, I did believe he was the type of fellow who would speak well of our religion to other Thai people and, therefore, found it very worthwhile to take the time to teach him. My total time in Lumphoon was six months, and other than the first month there, I was able to teach him on a fairly regular basis.

Of course, there was one small exception to that process. Khumnung had to take a month and a half out of his own life to be a Buddhist monk, as one of his relatives had recently died and his mother was ailing. Serving as a Buddhist monk required Khumnung to shave his head, don an orange robe for approximately six weeks, and pray and meditate at the local Buddhist temple on a full-time basis.

Thai culture and tradition were integral parts of everyday life for a missionary. Elder Warner and I proceeded out on a typical tracting path one fine morning only to get completely soaked with buckets and buckets of water. Our astonished looks must have tipped off one of the pranksters, who explained to us that *Songran (SOAN-grahn)* had begun. Songran is the celebration of the Thai new year and it is known as the Water Festival. For a three-day period of time, everyone sprays everyone else with water. Any serious business that was to take place in Lumphoon would simply have to wait until the Water Festival was over. There was nowhere you could go to escape the festivities. Life was celebrated while work was put on hold.

We were advised of a parade that was to take place in Ban Sang. Elder Warner and I decided to venture out to the parade to witness the holiday festivities there firsthand. This being a small village, the parade route stretched approximately one-half mile in length, which constituted the entire business section of Ban Sang. The street was lined on either side with two-story buildings that typically housed a small business concern downstairs and the business owner's family upstairs. Many of these structures had plumbing that included an outside faucet to which hoses were attached for the purpose of squirting parade watchers and participants alike. I got the feeling that, had we come to visit Ban Sang any other day, we would not see any hoses along the parade route.

As we viewed the parade, our conspicuous white skin, our conspicuous white shirts and ties, and our conspicuous height all combined to make us prime targets throughout the day. However, that did not mean that buckets and pails of water were not thrown indiscriminately at everyone who could be reached. It seemed that every second or third entry in the parade was a small pickup truck with at least two full barrels of water in the back, and with eight to ten people dipping buckets into the barrels and then emptying the water from the buckets onto the crowd. The crowd would retaliate with buckets full of their own water and streams of water from their hoses.

I could not understand how the various bands that performed in the parade could play any music at all while being drenched by the celebrants. Neither could I figure out how the Thai dancers could keep in step. I will never forget the last entry in the Ban Sang Water Festival parade. About twenty-five men dressed in bright-red leggings and Chinese-style shirts passed by, all playing various percussion and horn instruments. The bright red costumes fit none of the drunk musicians, and their black-and-white high-top Converse tennis shoes created a wondrous contrast between the old-world costumes and the new-world sneakers. I don't think I have ever seen a group of grown men act so disgustingly out of control and completely happy about it.

When the last entry passed by, you could hardly tell that the parade had ended. The streets simply filled up with spectators and the water fights continued unabated. Elder Warner and I did not hand out any tracts that day, nor did we present any first discussions to anyone, but we did have fun.

A zone conference was approaching for the twenty or so missionaries working in northern Thailand, and several elders began to ask me if I thought that I would ever become a senior companion. Frankly, I had not given it much thought, but upon reflection realized that I was probably one of the oldest junior companions in the mission and maybe even in the world. I really did not seem to mind. My senior companions, Elders Peckham, Kirby, and Warner, all had been very easy to get along with, and so I did not see any need for me to be in charge. But when I arrived in Lumphang, the site of our zone conference, my status as junior companion and the length of my stay in Lumphoon was a fixed topic of discussion.

In the mission field, elders are always prone to speculate about upcoming changes in the missionaries' assignments. It seemed I had been a junior companion in Lumphoon for so long that it was the consensus opinion that it was my turn to go. I had enjoyed my six months in Lumphoon, but did believe that I had seen about everything there was to see and probably had met almost everyone there was to meet, too. Some three months prior to the conference, I had even planted watermelon seeds and was closing in on the harvest of my one and only watermelon that was ripening on the vine in the front yard of the house. Perhaps it was time to move on.

XV

LIZARDS

I always enjoyed the missionary conferences. President Morris was an inspiration. Very much a leader who wanted to accomplish the tasks at hand; he meant business and I always knew that. On the other hand, he was always personable and understood that we were here to have joy in our lives and that the prospect of finding joy was not suspended simply by participating in a mission. Consequently, he seemed always to command the greatest respect from the missionaries in his charge.

President Morris's influence has stayed with me long since those days in Thailand. I even remember the gist of his conference remarks at the zone conference in Lumphang in 1974. He had observed the lumyai groves as he approached Lumphang. The lumyai fruit is somewhat smaller than a peach but grows in large numbers on each tree. The branches had become so heavily laden that the Thai farmers had to prop the branches up with lengths of wooden two-by-four's or bamboo. Otherwise, the branches would have broken from the weight of the fruit.

President Morris told us that his observation of the support required for the branches of the lumyai tree reminded him of the biblical story of an aged Moses who was presiding over a battle with the Israelites' enemy. So great was Moses' power that whenever he raised his arms, his Israelites would prevail. However, Moses' arms became so tired that he needed people to come and literally hold up his arms. By doing so, the children of Israel successfully vanquished the Amalekites.

In the same manner, we as missionaries needed to be supportive of our companions in order to achieve our goals in the mission field. By supporting each other, we would find that we would be helping ourselves. Without that support for each other, our missionary efforts would fail.

I oftentimes think of that talk even now and find it applicable to families, to team sports that I have played and coached, my business endeavors, and even my marriage. President Morris got me to keep this principle of service in mind simply by painting a mental picture of the lumyai tree and the fruit that it would provide if it were supported. President Morris's support of our missionary efforts was constantly evidenced by his listening ear and his advice and follow-through.

This was quite a contrast to the experience of a friend of mine who was laboring virtually simultaneously in the Philippines Manila mission. Elder Craig Fife was one of fifty or so missionaries participating in his own conference that was to be addressed by one of the Twelve Apostles of the church. First of all, it must be understood that Mormon missionaries are trained to be God's soldiers in the harvesting of God's children and in the fight against evil and that the Prophet and the Twelve Apostles are akin to the generals in God's Mormon Army. A visit, therefore, by one of the generals is something to be greatly desired and anticipated. The missionaries in Manila were very typical of those you would find anywhere else in the world. They all waited eagerly at the door of the chapel for the entrance of an apostle of God.

As the apostle entered the doorway, he appeared somewhat agitated at the elders clamoring forward to shake his hand. He moved up the aisle and took his place on the stand. Once the meeting was opened and the apostle was introduced, he rose to address the young missionaries, ready to do virtually anything he asked them to do. Instead of championing the cause, however, the apostle took the opportunity to chide the missionaries for not properly showing respect to him in his calling as an apostle. He then instructed the elders that when an apostle comes into the chapel, the elders were to stand in their places until the apostle had taken his seat at the head of the congregation. Once he sits down, then they may be seated. Elder Fife relates that particular apostle lost some thirty or forty supporters that day.

Upon hearing that story of form over substance, I could not help but contrast that nit-picking attitude to that of Jesus Christ and His Twelve Apostles. There are no rules of protocol in the New Testament about how people should behave in the presence of the Master. In fact, when children clamored for Christ's attention and they were rebuffed for their efforts, Jesus Christ put forth His hand and said, "Suffer the little children to come unto me, and forbid them not: for of such is the kingdom of God" (Mark 10:14).

True leaders do not need to rely upon form to extract respect. True leaders are rewarded for their leadership with respect. President Morris was just such a leader. The missionaries looked forward to seeing him. While on my mission, I just assumed that all mission presidents were like that. Later, I learned that my assumption was very incorrect. There are mission presidents like President Morris, and I was lucky to serve under him, but there are also other mission presidents who are patron saints of form over substance.

Following the conference, the missionaries were allowed to play a football game in the monsoon rains. Burning energy through sporting events has always been one of my favorite pastimes, and I was dressed and ready to play almost before the closing conference prayer was over. As I walked out the door toward the playing field, I noticed that most of the other missionaries were still in their white shirts and ties and were snapping pictures of President and Sister Morris. President Morris looked out of the corner of his eye and saw me, and turning to me said, "If you ever want to be a senior companion, Elder Palfreyman, you had better get your camera and come over here and take my picture!"

All had a great laugh and the picture-snapping elders put down their cameras, having gotten the president's message, and went in to change for football.

Upon returning to Lumphoon, it was rather depressing to learn that our best contact, Sister Phatcharaphon, had moved to Bangkok and that two of our other very good contacts, Warut *(Wah-ROOT)* and Warit *(Wah-REET),* had been admitted to the university for graduate studies, also in Bangkok. We had lost our three best contacts within a week of the zone conference and would now basically have to start over in grooming a new set of potential members.

There was no good location for a street meeting in Lumphoon and, after reviewing the matter for some time, Elder Warner and I decided that it might be fun to hold an open house. The planning began, and we spent the next two weeks working fervently to put together an open house that would attract as many people as possible from town to our home. We gathered filmstrips and picture books from Chiang Rai *(Chee-ANG Rai)*, Lumphang, and Chiang Mai and built a display of the Mormon version of the Plan of Salvation[13]. It depicted the pre-existent world, the earth, the judgment, and the three degrees (or levels) of heaven[13]. Display boards were prepared explaining the restoration of the gospel through Joseph Smith, and continuing modern-day revelation through existing prophets and apostles. Posters were drawn and brochures were printed up. All this took time and a great deal of effort, but both Elder Warner and I were satisfied this might well provide us with an introduction to new contacts for teaching purposes.

As the day of the open house drew near, I was advised it was my time to go to Cambodia again to renew my visa. One of the larger disappointments of my mission was not being able to see the open house through. This particular trip to Cambodia was somehow not as fun as any of the others. I couldn't help but think about what I was missing in Lumphoon.

On my trip back to Lumphoon from Cambodia, I stopped for the evening in Lumphang with Elders Welling and Brown, among others. That evening, I was advised of a truly remarkable event which brings a smile to my face whenever I think of it. Elder Brown was a missionary from Phoenix, Arizona, who was quite fun loving and one of the more upbeat missionaries I ever met. The Lumphang district of elders was rather downtrodden, as the work was not going well. Elder Brown tried several things to perk the other elders up, but nothing seemed to work.

One evening, as he was lying on his bed watching the lizards crawl across the ceiling over his head, he came upon an idea that he believed would surely lift the other missionaries' spirits. Elder Brown offered to eat the head of one of those lizards for ten dollars. After some negotiating, it was agreed that the other missionaries would contribute the sum of five dollars to a pot that would be payable to Elder Brown if he, in fact, ate the head off one of the lizards. Elder Brown then stood on his bed, reached up to the ceiling, and captured his meal. Without salt or other seasoning, and without cooking or even killing the creature, Elder Brown placed the head of the lizard into his mouth and crunched off the head. After a few bites, he swallowed, and it was over. Elder Welling was a witness to the event and said that he laughed himself sick. Another elder in the district also reacted by becoming sick, but did not laugh. He just got physically and violently ill.

Upon seeing the reaction to his prank, Elder Brown became concerned that he had acted in a light-minded manner, which would constitute a violation of his temple pledge. He wrote a letter to President Morris, reporting that he had something serious to confess. Before making a trip all the way up to Lumphang from Bangkok, President Morris apparently called to find out what he could about the confession that was to be forthcoming. He was filled in on the transgression and was relieved that it was nothing more than that. He simply advised Elder Brown to try and act in a more circumspect manner in the future. Years later President Morris shared his thoughts about the incident. Elder Brown's confession turned out to be rather minor compared to what could have been. The President's relief was almost overwhelming. He wanted to laugh but realized that Elder Brown had really regretted his unchristlike behavior so he too had to treat the matter seriously.

Moves came out on June 12, 1974, three days after my "hump day," a term referring to the half-way point in a mission. I was finally moving from Lumphoon and returning to the Bangkok metropolitan area. This time I was to work in Samsen. My companion was to be Elder Ricks and the two of us were responsible for a district that included some five million people, a dramatic departure from my experience in tiny, rural Lumphoon.

XVI

FLOPHOUSE

Samsen was a totally different world for me from what Lumphoon had been in many ways. Over the six-month period of time I was in Lumphoon, I met almost everyone in town at least once, and some two or three times. But in the Samsen district, Elder Ricks and I were charged with proclaiming the gospel of Jesus Christ to some five million people. That, in and of itself, was a bit overwhelming. Add to the fact that this was my first assignment as a senior companion and district leader (admittedly, a two-man district isn't all that challenging), and I felt I had landed smack dab in the middle of a great pit of quicksand.

Upon arriving at the apartment in Samsen, I was handed a stack of forty or fifty referral slips. Each referral slip represented an individual who, at one time or another, had come in contact with some aspect of Mormondom. These referral slips come from all over the world. Sometimes, they are filled out by members who have friends and acquaintances who they feel would be worthy candidates for membership in the church. Other times, the individual himself fills out the guest register at a Mormon church facility, such as a temple visitors center, or the Polynesian Cultural Center in Hawaii. Some of the referrals were more than a year old, and President Morris charged me with looking up every single one of them.

My companion Elder Ricks was an extremely quiet fellow from Idaho. It is strange that some forty years later I can hardly remember much about Elder Ricks, except that he had a very large appetite, said very little, and smiled even less. Having said all that, he was not such a bad guy; it just seemed clear in my mind that he would have been much more comfortable to be back home on his farm in Idaho. He was brand new to Thailand and seemed to be suffering from a bit of culture shock. Many missionaries experience culture shock due to the newness of language, crowds, and culture. As time goes by, adjustments are made, and most missionaries seem to assimilate just fine, like me (he said modestly). Elder Ricks was me, just one year removed.

I had never lived in Bangkok before and, at least at that time, there was no such thing as a *Thomas Guide* street map. Finding addresses was daunting to be sure, but did give me an opportunity to see parts of Bangkok that I otherwise never would have experienced.

Just as I had surmised, each referral we looked up presented a new adventure in travel. Addresses usually referenced a large main street such as Din Daeng *(Din Dang)* or Sukhumvit *(Soo ʌum-VIT)* roads. These roads were several miles in length each, but did at least refer you to a starting point. A *soi*, or minor street, then was referenced in the address and, for the most part, was an offshoot of the major road. Unfortunately, it was oftentimes impossible to tell by the address which end of the major road the soi was located on.

Looking up the referrals with the street address system the way it was, compelled Elder Ricks and me to spend a great deal of time chatting with people on the streets of Bangkok. One such trek was quite memorable. We had spent over an hour trying to find soi Rot *(Roat)*, which was off of Din Daeng Road. It was raining and we were both soaking wet. Monsoon rains are never drizzles. Lining the street that we were on was a row of small storefront businesses with, for the most part, dwellings located on the second floor above businesses below. Between the first and second floors, a thin concrete awning protruded over the sidewalk to provide shade during the hot season and protection from the monsoon rains during the rainy season. As Elder Ricks and I progressed along in front of this particular row of stores, we handed our referral slip to a young man who was seated in a folding chair outside the door of an unknown place of business.

I asked, "Do you know this address?"

He responded by shrugging his shoulders, and then after a moment said, "Wait here a minute; I will ask inside."

It had been a long day, and after waiting for several minutes, I turned to Elder Ricks and suggested that we follow our referral slip inside to see what had happened to it.

Upon entering the somewhat darkened room, my eyes lit upon a very curious business enterprise, one that I did not immediately comprehend. The room we had entered was large and spacious, with four or five rows of folding chairs, approximately eight chairs to a row, on the left side of the room. Four or five young Thai men were seated in the chairs seemingly at random, and were all facing straight ahead. I turned to my right to see what they were looking at. There was a very large pane of glass that was fully illuminated. Beyond the glass, I observed a broad staircase, some fifteen to twenty feet wide, including maybe a dozen stairs. The stairs were adorned in deep sculpted red carpet. Seated on the carpet were some fifteen to twenty women, all dressed in white dresses. It looked like a nurses convention of some kind, except for the fact that each of the women was sporting enough makeup to do Tammy Faye Baker proud. Besides the white dresses, the girls also shared a very unusual accessory. Bright red round pins, approximately three inches in diameter, were prominently displayed on the right chest of each of the girls. Each pin bore a separate and distinct number.

Elder Ricks came up to me and asked, "What is that?"

I was a little irritated that I still could not find the young man who had taken our referral slip and curtly responded, "How would I know?"

With that, one of the young men seated in the folding chairs to my left got up and walked to the far end of the room, where for the first time I noticed a cute young cashier in a glass box, much like a ticket taker in a booth at a movie theater. This young man walked up to the booth and asked for Number 21. The cashier then reached up over her head and pulled down a microphone, and then repeated the number, 21.

I then noticed that our little friend with the referral slip was standing next to the cashier, and so I headed his way. As I started towards the cashier and our little friend, I noticed that one of the girls in her white dress had gotten up and was moving towards the end of the glass by the cashier. She was wearing the pin with the number 21 on it. It was only then that I finally realized we were inside one of Bangkok's infamous brothels. I hurried over to our little friend and grabbed our referral sheet, mumbling some kind of apology for being so abrupt. I then turned and grabbed Elder Ricks and hustled him out of the joint.

Outside, it was clear that Elder Ricks was still completely in the dark about where we had been. I don't think I ever enlightened him. I was not too sure I wanted anyone to know that within the first week of being a senior training companion I had taken my charge into a brothel.

The experience was discouraging, but I had become somewhat obsessive about looking up each and every one of these referrals. In the weeks ahead, we did in fact crisscross our way back and forth across virtually every major road and many of the sois, along with some of the remaining canals in our little world, tracking down potential converts. It was actually a very good time. While our chasing of these referrals did not always result in meetings with our targets, frequently we would incidentally meet other people whom we could teach.

My most exciting incidental meeting occurred at a bus stop at a traffic circle at the Victory Monument. I could not believe my eyes when I jumped off a bus and almost into the arms of Sister Phatcharaphon, whom I had spent so much time teaching in Lumphoon. When she recognized which dumb American had almost knocked her over, she was equally surprised, and her remarkable eyes confirmed that she too had met up with a long-lost friend. I got all the particulars of Sister Phatcharaphon's new address in Bangkok, where she was working, and what her experiences had been so far in Bangkok. For her, Bangkok was a big city, too big. But she was enjoying her work and meeting with some of her extended family who lived in Bangkok. She had not seen them in many years.

I explained to her where the church was and asked if I could have the missionaries who lived in her area contact her so that she could continue taking the missionary lessons. She readily agreed and promised that she would see me Sunday morning at church. Sister

Phatcharaphon was true to her word and became a very welcome regular at church.

The makeup of the church in Bangkok was extremely different from what I had experienced in Lumphoon. In Lumphoon it was counted as a success if Elder Warner and I would go downstairs Sunday morning to find three or four investigators in our living room ready for church services. By contrast, Sunday meetings in Bangkok meant a trip to the only Mormon chapel in Thailand on Sukhumvit Road at soi Asoke. It was a small chapel by comparison to my experience at home, but easily would hold up to one hundred parishioners for a meeting. Surprisingly, the chapel even filled up on occasion. The Thai hymnal was quite abbreviated, and therefore the same songs were repeated over and over again. Regardless, it certainly was great to hear voices other than Elder Warner and myself sing the religious hymns that I grew up with. And hearing the hymns in Thai was an almost spiritual experience all by itself.

The Bangkok branch of the Mormon Church in those days included some of the most wonderful people I have ever met. Sister Kularb *(GOO-lob)* was a university student. She was enthusiastic about her studies, as well as about the church. She and I became fast friends, and she became a pipeline for American books of literature. She was studying English literature. *Connecticut Yankee in King Arthur's Court, Utopia,* and *Catcher in the Rye* were among the many books that I read during this time. The American humor of *Connecticut Yankee in King Arthur's Court* seemed to be lost on the very bright mind of Sister Kularb, while the political message of *Utopia* and the cultural observations of *Catcher in the Rye* were carefully dissected and analyzed. Discussing life through the eyes of the authors of the books Sister Kularb provided me with was akin to being back in college. I loved it.

Brother Awirutt *(Ah-ree-ROOT)* was another college-student member of the congregation. Typically Thai, in that he was extremely thin and wiry, his interests in spreading the good word that the church had to offer was quite genuine. Brother Awirutt would often accompany Elder Ricks and me when we would travel to people's homes to teach them. His actions as an intermediary truly smoothed the way for us to create a comfortable teaching environment.

A most attractive member of the congregation, as far as I was concerned, was Sister Nianna *(NAI-ah-nah)*. Not only was she naturally attractive, but she also was blessed with one of those captivating smiles that you simply could not ignore. Sister Nianna was another college student who would only be with us temporarily, as she was headed to college in the United States. Sister Nianna's hair, unlike most Thai women who let their hair grow long, was cut rather short, which was clearly intended to accentuate her high cheekbones.

I remember Sister Nianna always emphasizing that it was important for the missionaries to understand the Thai culture, so that we could better relate to the people we were trying to teach. One of her efforts in that regard was to take several of the missionaries on a little trip which the Thais would call a *tiaw (TEE-oh)*. A *tiaw* was anything you would do with friends or family away from home, such as an evening at the movies, a day at the beach or in the mountains, or a month in Europe. Missionaries were oftentimes told that their appointments with prospective members had to be cancelled because their appointment had gone on a *tiaw*.

Sister Nianna hosted such a *tiaw* to Ayutthaya *(Ah-YU-tee-ah)*. Ayutthaya was one of Thailand's historical capitals. Its ruins were a source of great pride to the Thais, as they were clear evidence of a very sophisticated culture that had existed for several centuries.

There were nine of us who journeyed north from Bangkok, including Sister Nianna. The ruins were every bit as spectacular as we had heard they would be. Large statues of Buddha were everywhere. The headless statues reminded us all of a rather dark moment in Mormon missionary history in Thailand.

We had no missionaries in Ayutthaya at the time of our visit, even though it was a substantially larger city than some of the other cities where we were then currently proselyting, such as Lumphoon. About eight months prior to my arrival in Thailand, two Mormon missionaries had been arrested for desecrating a statue of Buddha in a nearby town called Sukhothai, the first Thai capitol founded in the twelfth century. The version of the story that I have been able to piece together was that two missionaries serving in Nakhon Sawan, along with several other missionaries, and the Mission President and his wife, were all part of a mission conference in Phitsanulok. A side visit to Sukhothai was a part of the conference activities. A couple of the missionaries rented bikes and proceeded to visit ruins and the architecture in the area. Large stone statues of Buddha were everywhere and in one location, the missionaries were quite alone. They got a bit adventurous and one of them climbed up onto the lap of one of the giant Buddha statues. That not being adventurous enough, he then climbed on to the head of the Buddha and had his picture taken. When the film was developed, the owner of the photo studio was incensed and sent the photo to several newspapers throughout Thailand. The uproar caused no small stir and the offending missionary was arrested and sentenced to one year in prison for desecrating a holy site. Because he admitted the wrongdoing, his jail sentence was cut in half. The involved parties and everyone else who knew anything about the incident were all sworn to secrecy, which exacerbated the guilty feelings and mystery of the event. The missionaries involved felt plenty of guilt about letting the mission of the church down in Thailand. The incident was used as an instruction device over and over again to make sure that missionaries that followed behaved within the bounds of prescribed behavior rather than like the nineteen- and twenty-year-old boys they were. Little thought seemed to be given to the anguish and guilt felt by the missionaries. This appears to be a real weakness of organized religion generally, where the concern of the organization takes priority over concern for the one. It doesn't make the religion untrue, but it does show that priorities can get pretty mixed up sometimes.

As a side note about pictures from a mission, I do remember one picture that was sent back to Thailand after being processed at home in the States. As a part of our *tiaw* to Ayutthaya, we traveled in covered pickup trucks that were used for public transportation. One of the elders had taken a picture of the back of another truck as it was traveling down the highway. It was a rather innocuous picture of several missionaries waving out of the back of the truck. However, upon closer inspection, you could see a young Thai man relieving himself off to the side of the road. While this was a common practice in Thailand, the observation nonetheless made for a rather comical diversion from the everyday workload and a lesson of circumspection.

My best recollection of such an incident occurred some months later, while I was standing at a bus stop just outside of Bangkok. A nice young couple, appearing to be in their early twenties, were waiting at a bus stop across the street, holding hands and chatting with each other. Without missing a beat, they both turned away from the street so that the male could relieve himself at the bus stop. What was most impressive to me about the incident was that he never let go of his girlfriend's hand. Even if I had had the chutzpa to urinate in public, I am not sure that I could have physically accomplished the task one-handed. We didn't take a picture.

Samsen was a wonderful place to work. There was no end of people to meet and teach. There were great members who befriended me, helped acclimate me to the culture of the people of Thailand, and actually went out with me to teach their friends and neighbors. Finally, there was no end to the culture and life experiences that went on around me.

XVII

THE GUN

S ome mission experiences were easier to manage than others. On one occasion, Elder Ricks and I had run down a referral only to find that the individual listed had moved. Our journey had placed us near a government housing project, in which literally thousands of people called home. As Elder Ricks and I looked into the project, it seemed like almost everyone was milling around outside of the project in the open areas. We walked right on in and introduced ourselves. At first, we played *ta graw* and simply chitchatted with the residents there. After a while, questions began to be directed at us as to what we were doing there. It seemed perfect.

I replied, "I am a missionary for the Church of Jesus Christ of Latter-day Saints and have come here to teach you about Jesus Christ and the Mormon Church."

With that, I unleashed my flip chart that was made up of various pictures depicting the life of Jesus Christ and the early history of the Mormon Church. A group of forty or fifty people packed tightly around Elder Ricks and me, as I began to sermonize about God being our Father and sending to us His eldest Son, Jesus Christ, who led a perfect life and then gave His life for our sins. I then turned to the picture of Joseph Smith in the flip chart and began to describe how God the Father and His Son, Jesus Christ, appeared to Joseph Smith and asked him to act as Their representative upon the earth back in 1820 in Palmyra, New York, U.S.A.

As I continued to speak, the crowd began to pack more tightly around me and increased in size to where it could have numbered anywhere up to one hundred people. I noticed a commotion somewhere out in the midst of the crowd some fifteen to twenty feet from me. That commotion made its way toward me and finally became visible in the form of an angry gun-toting Thai teenager. As he approached, he raised the gun and pointed it directly at me. In no time at all, he had sidled up alongside me and pressed the end of the barrel against my heart. He was shouting and raving, first that I was a CIA agent come to disrupt the peaceful Thai population, and then alternatively, that I was a communist hell-bent on inciting a revolution.

I was more than a little frightened initially, but then felt quite calm, presuming that if I were to be killed while teaching about God, my place in heaven would be assured. At that moment, I was prepared to meet God. With that thought in mind, I continued my story. A few more tense moments passed before several other Thais in the crowd grabbed hold of the raving lunatic and dragged him and his gun away. Thereafter, several people apologized for the outburst of their countryman and begged that I continue.

In contrast to the lunatic gunman were the many people I met in the Samsen area who were genuinely interested in the message that I brought to them. One retired major general for example, who still worked as a computer advisor to the military, was extremely fun to teach and forced me to be very organized about what I presented, both about my concepts of the Trinity and about the need for a restored Christian church.

One of the truly pleasurable things about teaching Mormon doctrine is the simple concept of the nature of God and man's relationship to Him. "As man is, God once was. As God now is, man may become" (Lorenzo Snow, fifth President of the Church).

I taught a simplistic notion that God truly was our spiritual Father and that our elder Brother, Jesus Christ, was sent to this earth to live a perfect life and die as a sinless martyr for our sins. In that way, we as the children of God could come to earth and learn about life's experiences firsthand, without the fear of being condemned to hell for making mistakes. Virtually any mistakes that we made along the way could be forgiven through the Atonement of Jesus Christ, the Son of the living God. It was such a simple and straightforward message that even those who had never been exposed to Christianity before could gain a basic understanding of the concepts in a fairly short period of time.

XVIII

THE FATHER AND THE SON

Because I taught predominantly Buddhists, I rarely had to contend with much of Christianity's confusing (to me) view of the Trinity as set forth in the Nicean Creed. I have never been able to understand how God the Father and His Son, Jesus Christ, could be seen as being one and the same person, particularly in view of dramatic instances where the Father and the Son interact, specifically at the beginning and the end of Jesus Christ's ministry on the earth. God the Father joyfully proclaimed at the baptism of Jesus Christ, "This is my beloved Son, in whom I am well pleased" (Matthew 3:7). Certainly, this does not sound like one person talking to himself or about himself. Further, Jesus Christ's plea in Gethsemane was even more clear in its evidence that while one in purpose, the Father and the Son were separate beings. "If thou be willing, remove this cup from me: nevertheless not my will, but thine, be done" (Luke 22:42).

Jesus Christ began His ministry by performing simple miracles (comparatively speaking), such as turning water to wine. Then, through prayer to His Father, and fasting, He grew and developed in spiritual power and strength, and the nature and breadth of His miracles correspondingly became more fantastic and unexplainable, until ultimately He actually raised the decomposing body of Lazarus from the dead. His training was complete. The Father was satisfied that Jesus, His Son, was ready for the crucifixion. Jesus, too, knew of His divine destiny and waxed strong in His capacities so as to be able to perform His ultimate task. Even so, at Gethsemane, in prayer to His Father, Jesus Christ asked if there was some other way to perform the task that He had prepared a lifetime for.

The sacrifice of Jesus Christ's sinless life for the redemption of all mankind was required, and Jesus Christ was raised up on the cross. This gruesome experience is one that, for some reason, Jesus Christ had to live through on His own without the support of His Father. In order to complete the task, the Father withdrew His spirit from His Son, and allowed Jesus Christ to experience the crucifixion on His own. This is clearly evidenced by Jesus Christ's exclamation, "My God, my God, why hast thou forsaken me?" (Matthew 27:46).

What could it have been like for the Father to step away from His Only Begotten Son in the flesh so that Jesus Christ could endure the pain of all the sins of the world by Himself?

The relationship between God the Father and His Son, Jesus Christ, is analogous to the relationship that I have with my own daughter Claire, and a particular lesson that she learned one summer when she was six-years-old. We began the summer with a joint goal that she would be able to swim on her own by the end of the summer. We began with the simple tasks first, learning how to kick from the side of the pool and then with the use of a kickboard. Claire then learned to use her arms to stroke and then learned to turn her head to the side to breathe during her stroke. All the time I was at her side giving her instruction and comfort and the emotional support she needed to proceed with her task. I imagine that much the same relationship existed between Jesus Christ and His Father.

Near the end of the summer, we were staying in Laguna Beach, California, and Claire and I took a walk down the beach to the Blue Lagoon condominium complex. There, we entered one of the pool areas. Initially, we only wanted to see how warm the water was. But as we both descended into the pool, we realized that the time had come for Claire to swim on her own. We had spent the entire summer preparing for this moment, and we both knew that she was ready. I stood at her side and held her on top of the water. I will always remember the look that she gave me as I was about to let go so that she could swim on her own. She was ready. But for a brief moment, she did not want me to step away; she did not want to have to act alone, for up to that time she had always had my assistance. Maybe that is what the Savior was thinking when He asked why His Father had forsaken Him. As we looked at each other, I could see that she realized she was ready and this was the moment. After that brief hesitation, she put her head down in the water and swam all the way across the pool, all by herself.

There are some moments in one's life that seem quite simple but teach you great lessons that never leave you. This was one of those moments. I got a slight view of what God the Father must have felt when He stepped away from His Son, Jesus Christ, with the thought in mind that His Son was well prepared. It was time for Jesus to perform His task and fulfill His own destiny. I also could see with much more clarity the apprehension that the Lord Jesus Christ must have momentarily felt as His Father withdrew His spirit from Him so that He could perform, on His own, the salvation of man. Truly, God the Father and His Son, Jesus Christ, are one and the same in purpose. One is not merely a manifestation of the other, but rather God the Son truly is the offspring of His Father.

XIX

THE PLAID SUIT

Yes, Samsen was a wonderful place to be. Elder Ricks was smiling a little more, and he had even begun to speak at our several street meetings we would hold two or three times a week.

He also began speaking more readily with the bus hops and other hotel workers at the several hotels where we would place brochures for the patrons who stayed there.

On the other hand, it just did not seem that Elder Ricks was ever going to be a city boy. One of our tracting areas was accessible most reasonably by walking across approximately fifty feet of two-by-eight planking. This planking had been laid out over a former canal that had, over time, become nothing more than an open cesspool. I had never seen anyone fall from the planking into the black abyss before or after Elder Ricks did. Predictably, he said nothing about his fall and the only hint of any reaction by him at all was that his contorted facial expression revealed that he was well aware of the hideous odor he had stirred up.

Fortunately, his fall only caused him to disappear into the black mush up to his hip. Unfortunately, as he raised himself back up onto the plank, there arose a stench that dwarfed anything I had ever experienced before. I immediately offered to return home so that Elder Ricks could bathe and change. The offer was readily accepted. We walked home, not wanting to foul the air of those who otherwise would be sharing public transportation with us if we rode the bus. Elder Ricks bathed and changed. I am not sure that I ever again saw that pair of pants.

As I approached the one-year mark in Thailand, I began to sense a comfort level that I had previously observed in the older missionaries. By now, the language was hardly a concern. I knew my way around town, and I was rather confident about my ability to do my job. I had heard most of the tough questions that would be asked of me as a missionary and knew that when I didn't have an appropriate answer, it would not be the end of the world.

The time came for Elder Ricks to be transferred. So, I dropped him off at the church house on soi Asoke, and then traveled to President Morris's home, where I picked up my new companion, Elder Low. Elder Low seemed like a stranger to me, almost as strange as the Thai people when I first arrived in Thailand. Now, the Thais seemed normal, and freshly minted missionaries seemed foreign. I took that as the most clear sign that I had actually arrived as a fully integrated missionary in Thailand.

Elder Low was Canadian, by way of Salt Lake City, Utah. He had a swagger about him that led me to believe he had been something of a ladies' man back home. This was later borne out by the fact that he would get more mail from female writers than any missionary I had ever known. In fact, after observing that my letter count from women had dropped to close to zero, Elder Low volunteered, "No missionary should go without some girl writing to him. How about if I get you someone to write to?"

I was incredulous. "What in the world would I do with a pen pal? Besides, how would you know which one to cut loose from your stable?"

Some two or three weeks later, he announced that he had just the girl for me to write to. Her name was LaDonna Dalton, and he produced pictures for my perusal and proceeded to provide me with a brief biographical sketch.

I had to admit that she was quite attractive and she seemed very interesting. The only way I could put the matter to rest with Elder Low was to simply agree that if she wrote to me, I would respond. From that point to the end of my missionary experience, I regularly received mail from, and corresponded with, Ms. LaDonna Dalton of Salt Lake City, Utah. I never did meet her upon my return to the United States, however, nor did I ever write to her after I got home. Strange that returning home somehow meant the termination of our long-distance relationship. She had seemed very nice.

Elder Low and I got along extremely well. He was not afraid to tell me when I was being ornery or overbearing. On the other hand, he was not afraid to admit that he had a lot to learn and was actually very enthusiastic about being in Thailand on a mission. Elder Low, being new in the country, spoke about as much Thai as I did when I came into the country. We had a lot to work on. One of our favorite excursions was to go to the Thai Daimaru *(Dai-mah-ROO)*, a western-style shopping mall that allowed us to wander up and down the concourse of shops and meet with as many people as time would allow.

One of our most successful introductions was for me to initiate a conversation by introducing ourselves and then explain, "My friend here, Elder Low, is new in the country and knows very little of your language. The best way to improve his language skills is to practice speaking Thai with people like you. Do you have a minute or two to spend with Elder Low?"

It was amazing how often Elder Low would then be able to sit down at a bench and practice his language skills by actually introducing a gospel theme to his new-found friend. We were able to generate several follow-up meetings with such contacts, and Elder Low was simultaneously able to jump-start his practical Thai language skills.

At the same time that we were wandering the Thai Daimaru mall, we were also placing brochures (called "tracts" in the trade) in several of the major hotels around town and attending street meetings at Sanam Luang, Victory Monument, and other natural gathering spots around the Samsen area, as well as participating in the age-old missionary ritual of tracting (going door to door). Our efforts did produce many follow-up meetings, most of which resulted in dead ends, but some of which provided us with tremendously interesting and varied personalities to teach.

Elder Low and I relished our weekly meetings with a Brother Sompop and his children. We were never able to teach his wife, who I supposed was very suspicious of our motives and believed that her life would be ruined if she listened to us, since it would constitute a betrayal of her Buddhist vows. Sompop had three small children, two boys and a girl. Our weekly lessons always involved spending a significant amount of time playing with the children, either before or after the lesson. Sompop was always very attentive to our messages and was particularly interested in trying to reconcile his Buddhist upbringing with the Christian teachings he was receiving at our hand. He was genuinely impressed that several fundamental principles espoused by Buddha were also found in Christian theology. I opined that Buddha must have been one of God's great prophets in Asia, which would have explained the close correlation in the teachings of the two theologies. Unlike many of the people we taught, Sompop was not afraid to attend our church meetings, and he even came to witness a baptism on one occasion.

At this time in Thailand, baptisms were somewhat rare and, therefore, were highly prized events when they did occur. Being a district leader, I had the responsibility to interview candidates for baptism. On one occasion I interviewed Sister Chuusii (*Choo-SEE*), who had been taught the discussions by Elder Snedeker in our district. The interview process had been established to make sure that those people joining the church were actually serious about their commitments to the gospel of Jesus Christ, as taught by the Mormon Church. As a result, I spent a great deal of time with Sister Chuusii going over what she knew about the church and its teachings. Elder Snedeker had taught Sister Chuusii over a period of months, and did not seem to have left a stone unturned. She was quite knowledgeable about our belief that Jesus Christ was the Son of God and that He came to this earth and lived a perfect life on earth before being sacrificed to atone for our sins. She also understood that through the Atonement of Jesus Christ we all had an opportunity to return to our Heavenly Father.

While I am not one to enjoy administrative procedures in the church, it was a very gratifying experience to meet with Sister Chuusii before her baptism and then actually attend her baptism with Elder Low and Brother Sompop. I felt as if I had taken a small part in touching someone's life for the good. It seemed only a matter of time before Brother Sompop and his children would also make the commitment to become members of the Church of Jesus Christ of Latter-day Saints.

Through tracting, Elder Low and I had met one of the members of the Leadership Council of the Worldwide Fellowship of Buddhists. I did not hold out much hope of convincing him to become a Mormon. On the other hand, it was great fun discussing theological principles with him. He was very intelligent and his questions were probing and pointed. He was genuinely interested in what we had to tell him.

I was always quite positive that his interest was not due to any spiritual yearning to come to a knowledge of any truth beyond what he had already found in his life. He was the only person I ever taught in Thailand for whom I actually had to prepare written outlines of what I was to teach. Prophets acting as God's voices on earth, the spirit world beyond the grave, and many other topics subjected me to not only a reconfirmation of my own doctrinal positions prior to my meetings, but also challenged my language skills because of the depth of the issues we covered.

Another contact, Brother An *(Un)*, was a pleasure to teach. He and his three army buddies had just returned from a stint in South Vietnam and had experienced some rather gruesome times. They left several of their friends dead in the jungles there. They had been working basically as mercenaries for the United States military, and our initial contacts with them revolved around political inquiries as to why the United States never could quite seem to commit to a wholehearted effort to win the conflict in Vietnam. I had no good answer for them except to join in their dismay about the equivocal way in which the war was fought. My own sense was that there wasn't any clear goal for what we were doing. What if we actually won?

What would we do with the country? There were no good answers, and I could only sympathize with them for the senseless deaths of their friends. It also made me think about the U.S. military men and women who were sacrificing so much.

Their questions did allow Elder Low and me to introduce them to Christian values of love and brotherhood, long suffering, and the Atonement of Jesus Christ. From there, we had many opportunities to teach Brother An and his friends. If nothing else, we were at least able to convince them that the Americans were not all simply warmongers out to indiscriminately kill whoever they did not happen to like at any given time.

Elder Low and I were teaching several people in addition to Brother Sompop and Brother An, but not all our time was spent fighting the good fight. We also knew how to have fun. At this time, Elder Montgomery was also in Bangkok in a part of the city called Yanawaa *(YAH nah-wah)*. He and his companion, Elder Val Knights, spent many a diversion day with Elder Low and me. Diversion day was much like recess in grammar school. It seemed like you could only take so much work and then you would have to take a break before you could go back to doing more work. That was diversion day.

Our diversion days were supposed to be Mondays from dawn to dusk. We did fudge on that somewhat. With Mondays planned, Elder Low and I would either travel to Elder Montgomery's house, or Elder Knights and Elder Montgomery would travel to our house on Sunday evening so that we could get an early start on Monday morning. Mondays were always terrific. There were basketball games to be played, movies to be seen, monuments and sights to see, and shopping to get done.

Even though we were very organized in trying to maximize our Monday time, we were not always very lucid in our judgment of what to do with our time or how to spend our money. Tailors in Bangkok were very inexpensive, as was cloth. Elder Montgomery and I decided one day that it was time to find the proper material for a presentable three-piece suit. Now, when we left the United States, polyester had become quite the rage. Flared pants were also in vogue, and plaid had recently recycled its way back into fashion. Combining all three of these criteria, Elder Montgomery and I searched all over Chinatown for two full Mondays, trying to find just the right material to make just the right three-piece suit.

Ultimately, we were successful in our pursuit—or at least we thought we were. A street vendor of cloth had presented to us a large bolt of brown-and-white-plaid polyester that we could purchase in a sufficient amount to make two three-piece suits, and a pair of pants for Elder Knights. After some negotiating, we had established a truly magnificent price and our prize material was finally in our possession.

The following Monday, we traveled to a tailor well known to the missionaries, Mr. Somsamai *(SOAM-sah-mai)*. He seemed very pleased to see us and was only too happy to tailor our three-piece suits just the way we described them to him. It took three weeks to properly outfit us in these new suits, but finally, Elder Montgomery and I were satisfied with the results.

Unfortunately, these suits turned out to be the best evidence of the fact that we had been in Thailand way too long to ever truly fit back into American society. Some years later at a dance at Brigham Young University, Jay Montgomery and I were surprised to spy each other from across the dance hall, sporting our matching treasured suits. We were pleased, but we were alone. The bottom line was that we looked more like Steve Martin and Dan Aykroyd, those wild and crazy guys from *Saturday Night Live,* than like two normal human beings. A year or so after that BYU dance, my wife and her mother threw away that suit, hoping I would never notice the loss. I did, but by then I had become enlightened enough to say nothing. Elder Montgomery's wife once declared to him, "If I knew you even owned a suit like that, I never would have agreed to marry you!"

Looking back, I now understand that the cloth vendor was not laughing *with* us as we told our silly stories, but was actually laughing *at* us for picking out such a material to make suits with. The tailor, Mr. Somsamai, had probably also been entertained by our bad taste. I suppose the best that can be said about those suits is that we had fun creating them, and that others had a good time watching us wear them.

Those days were quite busy, with Elder Low and I having as many as four teaching meetings per day. It was a fulfilling time...lots of people to meet, lots of things to do, and not very much time to do it all in. I don't remember ever just sitting in the apartment and wondering what to do. It was a much different situation from what Lumphoon had provided.

One Sunday, in fact, Elder Low and I actually greeted ten of our investigators as they came to church. While we were still not baptizing up a storm, we were creating an interest, and our efforts were being rewarded. I suppose the downside to all this was that, because we were so busily and happily engaged, we did not notice that Elder Low's physical condition was deteriorating. Ultimately, he came down with pneumonia and had to be hospitalized for a week.

I could not help but think back to the time that I was hospitalized for my surgery. My mother later complained that my malady had been diagnosed, surgery performed, and my recovery almost complete before she ever knew anything had gone wrong.

Elder Low's family would be experiencing the same scenario because of their separation from him. I felt sorry for them.

It just so happened that the same day Elder Low was admitted to the hospital, another group of brand new missionaries arrived from the States. One of them, Elder Nebeker, was loaned to me during Elder Low's period of convalescence.

I took Elder Nebeker tracting for a day and we met a woman who indicated that her husband might be interested in meeting with us, but that he was only available at 6:00 in the morning. Consequently, Elder Nebeker and I arose at 4:30 the next morning so that we could be out of the house at 5:00 and on our way back to this woman's house to meet her husband. Unfortunately, he had come home the night before only long enough to tell his wife that he was required to travel out of town that night. He was not home. What a downer of an initiation to missionary work for Elder Nebeker! We returned home and ate breakfast.

After breakfast, we then kept my previously scheduled appointment with a major general, Prakaan *(Brah-GAHN)*. My discussion with Prakaan was on the eternal nature of man and that ultimately, the acquisition of all truth would provide us with the requisite knowledge to achieve perfection. I thought for sure that this experience would drive Elder Nebeker crazy, as he could not possibly have understood a word we said.

However, we then went to Brother Sompop and I mentioned to Elder Nebeker what I was planning to teach. He volunteered to participate in the lesson by giving two of the concepts out of the discussions. I was shocked that Elder Nebeker presented his memorized material without a hitch. I was envious. The LTM had certainly done its job training Elder Nebeker. Back on the bus after the meeting, I marveled at his accomplishment.

Elder Nebeker said, "I've done a little bit of acting and I can memorize anything. My problem is that I could not understand any of Sompop's questions."

I certainly could sympathize with that sentiment. It took several months before I could actually converse with anyone in Thailand about much of anything. Instead, everything had been in pidgin Thai or given as a part of a memorized lesson. Still, Elder Nebeker was significantly better than I had been at the beginning stages of the mission experience.

The next day I decided to give Elder Nebeker a chance to practice his Thai in a more informal setting and took him to the Thai Daimaru, where I introduced him as a new missionary in Thailand in much the same fashion as I had previously done with Elder Low. While Elder Nebeker was engrossed in his language lessons, I spotted the North Carolina State University basketball team. I was absolutely entranced. One of the coaches told me that they were actually playing a game in town next week and that tickets were available. I immediately told Elder Nebeker that we were through practicing Thai for the day and dragged him to the Sports Authority, where I purchased tickets to the North Carolina State game. They were scheduled to play the Thai national team.

After securing my tickets, I found out from other missionaries that they were also interested in attending the game, and ultimately some dozen or so missionaries all sat on the front row to see North Carolina State beat the bejeebers out of the Thai national team. (North Carolina State had won the NCAA championship earlier that year.)

Unfortunately, nobody had consulted with us about when the game was actually to be played. It was not played on one of our diversion days, and therefore was technically off limits to us. We believed ourselves to be safe, since we did not think that President Morris was a basketball fan and would not be attending the game himself. Hence, he would be none the wiser.

Alas, at the missionary conference that was scheduled just a couple of days after the game, President Morris let us know that he was an avid reader of the *Bangkok Post*. He then held up the front page of the *Bangkok Post* and displayed the picture thereon of the North Carolina State basketball team beating the bejeebers out of the Thai national team. Sitting on the front row in the picture, he pointed out to us that there were at least a dozen white-shirted Americans in attendance. While he admitted that the picture was not clear enough to identify them precisely, he was quite sure that he was talking to several of them in the room. Sheepishly, we acknowledged our indiscretion and personally committed to be more responsible in the future.

XX

POLYGAMY

It was a great relief to get Elder Low back. Not that Elder Nebeker was a slouch…he wasn't. It was just that working with Elder Low had been quite comfortable and I welcomed his return, even though he still looked a little pale and lacked any real endurance. As we were into the rainy season, our first job was to procure some blankets to keep Elder Low warm at night. While we did live in a nice apartment, it was typically Thai, which meant that there was no heater, and sometimes you could almost feel the wind blowing through the walls.

Elder Low and I got back into the proselyting mode slowly. For the first couple of days, we avoided tracting and stayed mostly with keeping teaching appointments and going to street meetings at either Victory Monument or Sanam Luang.

These days, street meetings were even better than they were in the past. Sister Deng and Sister Mellott met us at most every street meeting. Sister Mellott was an attractive, tall, red-headed woman from Salt Lake City, Utah, and Sister Deng was a no-less attractive Thai sister. Together, they never failed to attract a crowd, though the crowd was not always interested purely in the pursuit of religious truths.

Anyway, both sisters belied the elders' initial fears about the inclusion of sister missionaries into the Thailand Bangkok Mission. Before the sister missionaries came to Thailand, the elders had a wonderful sense that we were the true pioneers serving God on the virtual outposts of Christianity. Word that the sister missionaries were on their way somehow made the elders feel as if the frontier was about to be domesticated. A sense of true grief over the arrival of the sisters was most clearly manifested by Elder Welling's "guess-the-weight-of-the-sister-missionaries" contest that preceded the sisters' arrival by a couple weeks.

I have never been able to put my finger on why young women mature more rapidly than young men. Maybe it has something to do with their biological makeup and the fact that women face the prospect of childbearing, something that medical science has not yet figured out how to pass on to the male population. This maturing process would seem to justify sending young women out on the mission trail at an *earlier* age than young men.

However, the Mormon practice is to send young women out on missions at the age of twenty-one, two years later than the young men go out. Such a practice seems to create a rather stark disparity between the maturity levels of the young men and young women in the mission field. (More recently, the minimum age requirements have been adjusted to 18 years of age for men and 19 years of age for the women).

Now that I have four daughters of my own, I wonder why my own daughters have to wait an extra year to embark on their own missions. One explanation might be that such a disparity creates a natural emotional barrier between the young men and young women missionaries so that the risk of physical (meaning sexual) contact between them is minimized. The only other reason I can think of for the distinction stems from cultural and historical roots in the Mormon Church itself.

Traditionally, young men are trained from an early age that at age nineteen they are to embark on a two-year mission for the church, that this calling is from God, and that it is the religious duty of all young men to commit to and fulfill a mission. Young women, on the other hand, are taught from their youth that their job is to remain pure and chaste so they can become "mothers in Zion." In other words, a woman's primary function is to bear God's children and raise them as good Latter-day-Saint children, while boys are to fulfill missions and then become patriarchs in their own homes.

Regardless of all the above, the arrival of the sister missionaries in Thailand was an emotional event for the male missionaries already there. As it turned out, almost as soon as the sister missionaries arrived in the country, the "guess-the-weight-of-the-sister-missionaries" contest was forgotten. These sister missionaries were able to pull their own weight, and then some, so to speak. The Thais were impressed by the sister's language abilities, maturity and message. Sister Deng attracted a great number of Thai people (including women) because she was Thai and Christian. It was quite a sight for Thai people to see a Thai Christian and even more unusual that the proselyting Thai was a woman. Together, the sisters were impressive.

The Samsen experience was dramatically different from my time in Lumphoon. The challenge in Lumphoon was to find things to do that would provide us with teaching opportunities; in Samsen, the challenge was how to allocate time. There was never a problem finding people to talk to, and, on top of that, existing programs in the small but vibrant church in Bangkok demanded time of their own.

On Sunday, I was able to travel to a real church and meet with real members who could give real talks and lessons. I wasn't responsible for absolutely everything that went on in a church meeting, which was a wonderfully relaxing feeling.

Family Home Evening would arrive every Monday night, with members taking turns giving the lessons. The Family Home Evening group was made up of members who were relatively young (college age) and single. Their camaraderie was very tight because their acceptance of Christian principles almost naturally separated them from many of their Buddhist friends.

Tuesday night's Elder Low and I traveled to the Asoke chapel to teach English, where we oftentimes would draw classes of up to thirty participants, almost all of whom were non-Mormons. The English lessons always had some kind of church theme. Some weeks we talked about Jesus Christ and His teachings, and other weeks we talked about the Mormon Church and its origins. One of the great things about teaching English in Bangkok was that Sister Phatcharaphon would come to class whenever her work schedule would permit it. It would always make my day to see her walk into the classroom.

After a time, Sister Phatcharaphon acquired at least some degree of seniority at her hospital and was able to attend church on occasion. The dedication of the church building in Bangkok was of great interest to all, and Elder David B. Haight, one of the Twelve Apostles, was to come to Bangkok and perform the dedicatory prayer. Elder Haight presided over a truly spiritual meeting and was as humble and gracious as you could ever hope to see. His genuine interest in greeting each individual Thai after the meeting had a truly positive impact in boosting the morale of the missionaries and conveying a Christian spirit to the Thai members and investigators. I have always remembered Elder Haight quite fondly since that time.

It seemed to me that almost all the work in Samsen was enjoyable. Meeting people was a breeze, and we always had at least a half a dozen non-member contacts we were teaching at any one time.

Sompop, however, continued to be a mystery. Whenever he was available to be taught, we had excellent lessons with him and his children. (His wife always stayed in a back room.) He would listen intently to what we said, asking questions when he did not understand. Then, astonishingly, he would turn and explain the concept to his children. I could not help but think that ultimately we would reel Sompop into the church. A strange thing about him though, was that he would regularly disappear and we would be told only that he was in another province.

After teaching Sompop and his children for almost four months, Elder Low and I believed we had finally come to the point where a serious discussion about baptism into the church was warranted. Elder Low and I prayerfully approached Sompop on the subject one rainy evening. We asked him about various specific doctrinal questions. He responded to our questions quite positively. Over time, he had become quite knowledgeable. He was willing to commit to baptism and the covenants that were involved with it. Namely, he was ready to accept Jesus Christ as his Savior, and in his heart, I believe he had already achieved a spiritual commitment. Other commitments that Sompop, as all other converts to Mormonism must make, seemed simple. He did not smoke, he did not drink, and seemed quite sure that giving up coffee would be no real problem. He also believed that he could adhere to the law of tithing, and then we got to the law of chastity ...

Sompop seemed to be a wonderful family man. I had always looked forward to coming to his house and meeting with him and his children, though I had found it strange that his wife never joined with us. She was pleasant enough in greeting us at the door, but beyond that, was quite reclusive. I asked Sompop if he could commit to having sexual relations with no one but his wife. It was only then that I learned the answer to the mystery as to where Sompop would so frequently disappear to. He responded to my question quite positively, saying, "Yes, I can commit to having sexual relationships only with my *wives.*"

By this point in time, I was very comfortable with the Thai language and I knew that Sompop had clearly said he would have sexual relations only with his two wives. But I just couldn't believe it, and so I asked him to repeat his response, which he did. It turned out that Sompop was maintaining two separate families at once. He was a polygamist. In the nineteenth century, he would have made a great Mormon. Unfortunately, we were not in the nineteenth century, and I could not baptize Sompop.

Polygamy had not only been an accepted practice in the Mormon Church, but an integral part of the religion throughout the latter part of the nineteenth century. Despite having to endure severe persecution, largely due to the practice of polygamy, the early prophets steadfastly held to the doctrine of polygamy, maintaining that it was part of God's eternal order of things.

Due to persecution, the Mormons were driven from the borders of the United States by religious bigots who sought to impose their own set of religious values on the Mormons. The Mormons ultimately settled and flourished in the then-obscure and isolated

Salt Lake Valley, in what was later to become the State of Utah. In isolation, the Mormons continued to practice polygamy until the westward expansion of the United States threatened. As a price for admission into the United States, the Mormon hierarchy banned polygamy by manifesto in 1890.

Immediately after the Manifesto of 1890, polygamists with high visibility were asked to actually give up their families to comply with the Manifesto. Others, who were able, simply disappeared from visible society so that they could maintain their pre-existing family relationships. Meanwhile, some ardent supporters of polygamy continued to perform polygamous marriages into the twentieth century. The practice of polygamy that Joseph Smith declared was ordained of God had been cut off by decree for political expediency. To this day, the principle of polygamy remains a viable tenet in the doctrine of the church. However, its practice is punishable by excommunication.

As a young missionary faced with the dilemma of Sompop, I was completely lost. Those I spoke with in the church advised me that he could not be baptized. I could not bring myself to ask him to abandon one of his families. What could I do? I was so lost that I ultimately did nothing. I never saw Sompop and his children again, and to this day I regret that fear and confusion carried me into total inaction in the matter. I surely let Sompop down.

XXI

CAMARADERIE

Mission conferences were always events to be looked forward to. Our mission conference this year took place on the Gulf of Siam near Chonburi *(CHOAN-ber-ee)*. The convention center was perched on a small spit of land elevated slightly above its surroundings. The atmosphere was that of a tropical paradise, and not since Hawaii and the LTM had I wanted to swim so badly. The waves were small and broke right on the sand. It became great fun to simply walk up to the very edge of the ocean with the water up to the mid-calf line. If you ducked down low enough, the waves would break right over your entire body, and the sensation was sinfully delightful.

After wrestling, playing catch, and joking with all my old missionary friends, we enjoyed a program of several skits put on by the various missionaries. Clearly, there was a wide divergence in talent ranging all the way from me, who had no talent at all on stage, to Elder Pitt, who actually composed music and wrote words to what became the unofficial mission song in Thailand.

To this day, I can remember the words to the first verse. They were wonderful:

Mud on my cycle, Dust on my slacks,
Riding around old Lopburi *(LOAP-ber-ee)*
Hand'n out them tracts. I'm tired and I'm dirty
And all they say to me
Is, *"Sasanaa thug sasanaa son Hi khon ben khon dii."*
(All religions teach men to be good)

Elder Pitt's song was such a hit that it was sung over and over again. It captured the essence of the daily grind of being a missionary in Thailand. It was hard work. It was dirty work. For the most part, we were met with very little real success. People simply dismissed us by saying that all religions were basically the same, and so it didn't matter which religion they practiced. But the song assured us all that we were not alone.

This conference was held during the high rainy season, and so, true to form, there was a steady downpour every day of the three-day conference, though it did not have any impact on the spirits, the messages, or the companionship we all shared at the conference. Further, the rains provided us with the most entertaining part of the entire conference. When it came time to leave, for the first time, we all realized that the road which brought us to the conference, and was to take us back home, had disappeared under two to three feet of water.

One of the nicest things that could happen to this missionary was that he would be required to go into the water. With our bags packed and hoisted up onto our shoulders, we all began to make the trek along the roadway, which was under water and not visible for a hundred yards or so. On either side of the roadway were rice paddies that were somewhere between four and five feet under water. There was a fairly hefty current flowing from north to south across the roadway, and all in all, it made for a perfectly enjoyable crisis for some fifty to sixty nineteen- and twenty-year-old boys. One mischievous elder actually dropped his softball into the water and watched as it floated away from the line of missionaries. He then handed his duffel bag to his companion and exclaimed, "Hold this; I'll get that ball!"

He then made a less-than-graceful dive into the current to retrieve the ball. He was cheered on by all. Many of the cheers, like mine, were more for his ingenious ploy to get into the water than for the actual rescue of the softball.

There was one moment at the conference that was rather disturbing to me. It was when I was told I would be moving on to a new home. In the four months that I was in Samsen, I had grown accustomed to a very wonderful life: a great companion in Elder Low, wonderful members, five million potential investigators of the church, basketball games against all the colleges and universities in Bangkok, and the camaraderie of the many elders who were then stationed in and around Bangkok. I would sorely miss all of that. There are some things in life that you wish you could change, but you cannot. This move was one of those things.

XXII

RABID DOGS

Even though Nonthaburi was just a one-hour bus ride from downtown Bangkok, it had a feel similar to Lumphoon. It clearly was a distinct suburb, and the pace of life there was much more relaxed and slow than the energy I felt in Samsen. But I guess that wasn't all bad, particularly since I was now in a four-elder district, which gave me two more options for people to talk to than I had had available to me in Samsen. I look back and think how lucky I was that Elder Ricks and then Low were my companions in Samsen. A two-man district can be pretty lonely.

In Nonthaburi, I was assigned to Elder Probert. At the time of the assignment, I was told that I should go slow with Elder Probert, and that if I was patient, he would come around all right. It turned out President Morris knew more than he was volunteering to me. Elder Probert was about 6' 1" in height and weighed somewhere in the neighborhood of 220 pounds. Rumor was that he had played football for Brigham Young University before coming to Thailand as a missionary. His mind always seemed to be in some other time zone. There was a part of Elder Probert that required him to pray. He was always on his knees, which meant we were late to almost everything.

I have never been the greatest at getting up in the morning. So having to prod Elder Probert to finish praying each morning was a chore that I was not too sure I was up to. But more than that, our 8:30 a.m. appointments had to slowly be pushed back, first to 9:00 and then to 10:00. It wasn't so much that we couldn't get up and dressed in time; it was just that Elder Probert would not get off of his knees. It seemed that he would rather pray than do anything else.

After missing several appointments completely, I finally called President Morris and asked what I should do. I said, "After all, President, we do believe that he is praying to God and I certainly don't feel right about interrupting him if that's really what's going on. On the other hand, there is work to be done."

I always liked President Morris. He never seemed to be at a loss for a practical solution to virtually any given problem. The answer was simply for me to wait for Elder Probert downstairs in the chapel (our living room), and then after a time yell upstairs to him that it was time to leave. In that way, I would never have to actually acknowledge that Elder Probert was praying, and therefore, I would no longer be interrupting him. It almost seemed too easy, but it worked.

Now that we had gotten through the prayer problem, we just had to make sure he was dressed. Our four-man district would routinely be ready to pray our way into the day's activities immediately before leaving the house each morning. There I would stand with Elders Alan and Slater, waiting for Elder Probert. The three of us would shoot the breeze for a couple of minutes and then call Elder Probert down.

Elder Probert was the first experience I had with a missionary who seemed to be troubled about something in his life. It seemed that Elder Probert expected perfection from himself. The problem was that there is just no real way to be perfect in everything, especially with the language. He was already way ahead of me at his stage of his mission. It drove Elder Probert crazy, I guess. The long and short of it is that Elder Probert figured it out. He became a great missionary, significantly better than me, probably because he already was a better person than I was.

Another part of the Nonthaburi experience that was difficult for me to adjust to were the church meetings. In Bangkok, I would show up to church and enjoy the company of the members and investigators. My only specific job was to teach an investigator's class. I was in heaven.

In Nonthaburi, on the other hand, I was responsible for the administration of the church meetings. Sister Patcharin *(PUTT-chah-rin)* was my only active member. She was the Sunday school teacher. At twenty years old, single, and rather attractive, she was much more interested in traveling into Bangkok to attend church where there were contemporaries to associate with. Consequently, her attendance in Nontaburi was hit and miss. I could not blame her. Brother George also lived within the boundaries of our little congregation in Nonthaburi. He was our "dry Mormon." A dry Mormon is one who is not baptized (hence he is dry) but participates in virtually all the church activities and practices the church's cultural and physiological mores, as if he were a member. Alas, Brother George, too, liked his trips into Bangkok. I could not blame him in light of the passel of cute, single Thai women who attended the Bangkok branch. Anyway, administration really wasn't my thing.

Proselyting time was somewhat scarce during my first month in Nonthaburi and, strangely, I was missing it. I needed a change. What kind, I didn't know. I assure Elder Probert and all who may one day read this that I did not pray for the next event to occur, but it sure was a change. It was not any kind of change that could possibly be a good thing for poor Elder Probert.

Elder Alan, Elder Slater, Elder Probert, and I were following our customary practice of saying a brief joint prayer in front of our home (and the church) before we headed out for the day. On this one occasion, Elder Probert complained about a small, rather sickly looking pooch that was acting rather strangely as it paced around our circle. Elder Probert providentially viewed the dog as an attacker. To me, he looked strangely reptilian, like almost any other Thai dog I had ever seen...protruding ribs due to lack of food, hair only in patches on his back and sides, gaunt, and basically looking as if a strong wind would blow him over and kill him.

Since Elder Probert was nervous about the presence of the dog and the other three of us were rather anxious to get going, I asked Elder Probert to pray us out, thinking that praying would take his mind off of the dog.

No sooner had Elder Probert begun to pray than that dog attacked. It was so strange that he did not attack me or Elder Alan or Elder Slater; it was as if he had been assigned to seek and destroy Elder Probert. I didn't know a tiny dog like that could howl so viciously, and I certainly did not anticipate the grit and determination the dog displayed. It took several good swift kicks from all of us before the marauding dog finally let go of poor Elder Probert's leg.

Elder Probert looked down at his bleeding leg, and I thought he was going to freak out. At first, we assured him that it looked only superficial, and that he needn't give it any further thought. After some cajoling, Elder Probert changed his torn pants, and we were off to do what missionaries do.

The following morning, Elder Probert and I were teaching English to the landlord's children, when one of our neighbors hurried to our front door, looking extremely distressed. Without waiting to be invited in, Nurimon *(NER-ee-moan)* pushed open the door and blurted out that the dog which had bitten Elder Probert was "crazy." I thought so too, but had to refer to my Mary Haas Thai/English dictionary to discover that when a dog is referred to as crazy in Thailand, it means he is rabid. I then asked her how she knew this, and she explained that the dog had died the night before, foaming at the mouth and running itself into a metal security door several times before collapsing dead in the street.

This whole incident all of a sudden didn't sound too good to me, and I walked down the street to inquire further. Fortunately for Elder Probert, he was not yet proficient enough in the language to have caught on to what was going on. I told him, "I am going down the street to get some butter at the market. I will be right back. You keep on with the English lesson."

Upon arriving at the market, I confirmed the story about the rabid dog. The shopkeeper then asked if we as missionaries would be raising the five puppies that were now without a mother. Sure enough, I had forgotten all about the fact that this rabid dog was actually a mother of five and had been raising her pups in an open field next to our house.

After my own unsuccessful attempts to recover the body of the rabid dog, I then took Elder Probert into Prommitr *(PROAM-ee-ter)* Hospital to see what should be done. I was no medical genius... all I knew about rabies was that it was bad and that treatment for it was not pleasant. After telling our story to the doctors at Prommitr

Hospital, we were told that Elder Probert surely needed to go through a series of rabies shots. That meant one shot every day for two weeks. Unfortunately, Prommitr did not have the necessary serum. After being told at a second hospital facility that they also had no serum, I called President Morris with the news. He had some connections with the U.S. Army Hospital in Bangkok and assured Elder Probert that he could get him in there for the necessary treatment. It meant that Elder Probert would have to move to Bangkok for the next two weeks, and Elder Reed became my temporary companion in Nonthaburi.

President Morris had given me some disturbing instructions when I dropped Elder Probert off. I kept those instructions to myself until I returned home to Nonthaburi. I then shared with the other three elders in the district that the doctors at the U.S. Army Hospital had advised President Morris that the puppies quite probably had contracted rabies from their mother, and should therefore be destroyed. President Morris's instruction to me was to terminate the puppies. This wasn't the United States of America where you could just haul the puppies into the Humane Society and drop them off so they could be "put to sleep." Instead, I was supposed to kill them. I was at a loss for how to proceed.

The following evening, Elder Slater, Elder Alan, and I were engaged in our usual bottlecap-flipping exercises. This involved placing your thumb and middle finger together as if you were going to snap your fingers. You would then wedge a bottlecap in between your thumb and middle finger and hitch your hand back behind your ear. If you performed the snap properly and calculated the trajectory appropriately, you could launch a bottlecap for a good twenty-five to thirty yards. Immediately in front of our house was the remnant of a rather large canal that was thirty-five to forty yards in width. Our goal each night was to launch our bottlecaps all the way across the canal. No one was ever quite successful, but we got close.

On this one evening, as bottlecap after bottlecap fell short of its goal and into the canal, the thought came to me that we could simply drop the puppies into the canal. It seemed gruesome, but also quick and easy. I really had no other ideas to choose from anyway. So, I tested the depth of the canal by hurling a very large rock into its center. It clearly was deep enough to do the job. Next, I purchased a large burlap sack and a small length of rope. I then found a sufficiently heavy stone and placed it inside the burlap sack with the five puppies. After tying the top of the burlap sack closed, I hurled it for all I was worth so that it would make it to the center of the canal before splashing down. There was only one quick helpless yelp, and the deed was done. We didn't talk much about the incident after that, but I guess sometimes you just do what you have to do.

XXIII

BAD NEWS: SEEING THE END

had been playing basketball with Elder Reed for the last couple of months and looked forward to working with him every day. He was 6' 5" and no bean pole. Elder Reed was quiet but very happy about doing his job. I could assign Elder Reed almost anything. It was terrific. It could have been easy to get carried away with the concept of delegation.

Proselyting picked up almost immediately, and I again began to experience the good feelings that come with just going out and doing your job.

I first met Thiriphoon *(TEE-ree-pune)* at a street meeting about a week before Elder Probert had been bitten. Elder Probert and I had only met with him once since then, but he seemed to be quite interested. We just couldn't seem to get our act together enough to get out there and visit him because we just could not get out early enough in the morning. With Elder Reed, we were able to see

Thiriphoon three times over the next two weeks, and he actually began coming out to church.

Similarly, Sangob *(Sang-OAP)* was a fellow whom Elder Probert and I had tracted out on our way home from a no-show meeting that had been scheduled. He, his wife, and five children seemed like prime candidates for conversion. Unfortunately, we had not made much progress in the first month we had worked there. The arrival of Elder Reed helped to break the ice. Sangob and his family seemed to become interested in more than just the novelty of entertaining Americans. All our other contacts seemed to begin to blossom as well.

I was scheduled to return Elder Reed to Bangkok after two weeks and made arrangements to do so in conjunction with a church conference wherein all missionaries, members, and investigators throughout Thailand were to gather in Bangkok for one Sunday. Elder Reed and I tried to commit as many people as possible to attend, but you could never tell what kind of attendance you would actually get.

Elder Reed packed his little bag, and we bussed into Bangkok along with Elders Alan and Slater. Upon arrival at the church on soi Asoke, we were greeted by two or three of the investigators whom we had invited to the conference. By the time the conference actually began, thirteen investigators from Nonthaburi had made the trek into Bangkok. I can hardly begin to describe the sense of accomplishment I felt sitting in a rather small congregation and knowing that a good percentage of those in attendance were there as a result, at least in part, of our efforts.

As I sat in conference with my investigators, I tried to listen to the various speakers. I mean, you are supposed to do that. But my heart was not in it. Instead, I looked around at the congregation and saw so many of my good friends from my days in Samsen. For the first time since I left Samsen, I began to realize how much I missed them all. Then, almost immediately, it struck me for the first time that it would not be all that many more months until I would be going home, never to see most of these people again. I wept quietly through the rest of conference, trying to figure out what life would have to offer me at home that it hadn't already given to me in Thailand.

A few days after returning home from conference, I was in the local market picking up some sundries when I ran into a neighbor friend who happened to drive ten-wheeled trucks (the biggest trucks in Thailand at the time) on long hauls throughout the country. We got to talking about the neighborhood generally and then about that wild dog that had bitten poor Elder Probert. The truck driver laughed and then shared with me that he had heard that story about the rabid dog, but he could not bring himself to tell anyone in the neighborhood that he had actually run over the dog with his truck. In other words, that dog died because he was hit by a truck! It might not have had rabies at all! I never could bring myself to share that tidbit of information with Elder Probert. He had already been through enough.

XXIV

RESURRECTION

Thais are big into boxing and specialize in their own brand of kick boxing. I had purposely stayed away from such events, figuring somehow that as a missionary I should not be endorsing the pummeling of human beings, one against another. The Mohammed Ali vs. George Foreman fight in Zaire, Africa, however, seemed somehow different. No matter where we went, everyone talked about the upcoming fight. Was Mohammed Ali too old and out of shape? Was George Foreman just too strong?

Elder Probert and I spurned invitations to watch the fight at the breakfast hour at several people's homes, not getting the sense that it would be appropriate. If the truth be told, we did want to see the fight. I had remembered talking to some Thais about how Mohammed Ali had been doing thousands of sit-ups every day in preparation for the fight and thinking how woefully inadequate such training would be.

On the morning of the fight, I realized that there was just no way around it...I really wanted to see the fight. Elder Probert and I went in to town for breakfast and just happened to pick out an eatery that had a television tuned in to the big event. I doubt there were any televisions in Thailand that day that were turned on to anything else. The *guitio* (*GWEE-tee-oh*) was excellent, with a distinctively spicy taste. The first seven rounds or so of the fight stunk. Mohammed Ali simply curled up into a little ball, guarding his face and upper body with his arms and letting George Foreman pummel his midsection. I marveled that Mohammed Ali was able to come out for each round. But come out he did in the eighth round and, after about thirty seconds of laying on the ropes and acting as George Foreman's punching bag, Ali then viciously attacked the tired Foreman and rang his bell, in what was to become known as the famous "Rope-A-Dope" fight.

I had never been very interested in watching grown men beat each other up. But in this fight, for the first time, I watched an older, more worn man use his grit and intellect to chop down a much younger and stronger opponent. It was a good fight to see, missionary or no.

As time passed, Elder Probert's language skills were really improving, which was making my life a lot easier. He was also reaching a real comfort zone. I had concluded from my time with Elder Probert that I must be a great life coach. He just seemed to blossom during our time together. However, the real source of change probably had more to do with him realizing that being a good missionary wasn't all that hard if Elder Palfreyman could serve. I apparently set a low bar that Elder Probert could easily clear. So, can I take credit for that?

Somehow, the missionary work in Nonthaburi was going extremely well. Unfortunately, my friend from Downey, California, Elder Slater, had been transferred away. He was replaced by a new missionary from Salt Lake City by the name of Elder Jensen. Elder Jensen was rather quiet and, being brand new to the country from the LTM, he was in shock and, therefore, quite receptive to whatever Elder Alan wanted him to do.

The four of us had street meetings in town, two or three times per week, and tracted virtually every day. It became fun to receive a referral slip from Bangkok that was for a part of town we had not been to before. We could plan our day around finding the referral and then tracting that part of town. It seemed that Nonthaburi was almost virgin territory, which allowed us to routinely tract an area that had never been tracted before.

During one of our forays, we ran across a very promising looking Thai man with a very Western attitude. His wife and four teenage children were quite receptive to our message that Joseph Smith had talked to God way back in 1820, and that through Joseph Smith, God had set up a church that allowed His children to learn truths that would help them find joy in this life, and eternal peace in the next.

Sutchii *(Soot-CHEE),* his wife, and their children began to study with us every week. Our Wednesday nights, for the next few months, would find us always in Sutchii's home. Some nights we just chatted about daily living, and others we were able to focus on religious lessons.

On a couple of occasions, we simply sat and watched television together, as I would become mesmerized by the squeaky high-pitched Thai voice coming from the mouth of a hulking Hoss Cartwright from the "Bonanza" show. The contrast was so absurd that I just couldn't stop watching it.

With every visit to Sutchii, there was food, and lots of it. His wife was a superb cook, and consequently was not as lean as most Thais whom I ran across in Thailand. She was quite a contrast to her husband, who stood about 6' 2" and could easily have been mistaken for a javelin. Their home was typically middle class in appearance, with a tin roof covering thin walls of wood siding. The entire home was elevated some six feet from the ground, and the steps entering the living area spanned the full front of the house. In fact, when the front doors were open all the way, the steps were actually used as part of the living area.

Sutchii and his family were rather popular in the neighborhood, in light of their proud ownership of the only television set on the street. While it served as a deterrent to religious discussions on some occasions, it oftentimes served as a lightning rod to attract a good share of the neighborhood on some evenings, so that at times Elder Probert and I could spread our religious message to up to forty people in an evening. We were very consistent in always inviting Sutchii and his family and friends to church. They were just as consistent in their avoidance of our living-room chapel. Nonetheless, the visits went on and our friendship grew.

Along with Sutchii and his family, we were regularly teaching a dozen or so other individuals, each with their own level of interest and each with their own problems and concerns. At this time, almost three quarters of the way through my two-year tour of duty, the language had actually become fun, and therefore contacting and teaching had become as easy as an uncontested lay-up in basketball.

That did not mean that conversions were being racked up at any great pace. In fact, at the time, missionaries in Thailand could generally expect about one to two baptisms per mission, and about half of those did not remain active in the church for any substantial length of time after their baptisms.

As I got to know one of our contacts we called Brother George, I found him to be extremely affable and quite anxious to join the church. When he was not attending church in Bangkok, he was a great help to me in teaching classes at our church in Nonthaburi, and he also helped in our various proselyting efforts. The day of his baptism was greatly anticipated by a whole string of missionaries who had taught him before I got to Nonthaburi. Over the course of two years or so, Brother George must have been taught by twenty or more different missionaries. We made sure that all our investigators were invited to the baptism that would take place in Bangkok. Five showed up and were quite impressed with the symbolism of total immersion, which represented a complete washing away of all sins. In fact, Brother Anan *(Ah-NUN)* announced at the baptism that he too was ready to take the plunge.

Brother Anan was a very interesting old man. He had fought in World War II and Vietnam and was very thoughtful in his consideration of what we had to offer. At times, I did wonder about Brother Anan, as some of his observations would catch me off guard. One day, in Sunday school some two or three months before Brother Anan's own baptism, I was teaching a lesson on the resurrection. I explained that all of us as children of God would enjoy the fruits of the resurrection and that this gift was by the grace of God: it was His free gift to us.

Looking at the faces of those to whom I was speaking, I was quite satisfied that my message had been heard and understood. Brother Anan raised his hand, then stood and confirmed for me the principle of the resurrection. At least, I thought that was what he was doing.

He declared that he had been resurrected, and then explained. In Vietnam, he had been shot right through the chest. As he lay on the damp jungle floor, he felt his spirit leave his body, and then recalled looking down at his dead corpse and seeing that he was dead. As he related this near-death incident, he opened his shirt to show to all present, the remaining scar as proof of the incident. Now he was alive again, and therefore, resurrected. While I do not doubt that Brother Anan was speaking from his heart, I was keenly aware that we had not completed our discussion of the resurrection.

By now, the number of missionaries in Thailand had changed dramatically. It had gone from some forty-five missionaries when I arrived to somewhere in the neighborhood of one hundred fifty missionaries. I was considered something of a dinosaur, and had achieved the label of "old head." There wasn't anything really special that you did to obtain that title except survive. That I had done, along with most of my other cohorts from the LTM.

XXV

THE PRANK

Elder Montgomery and I still tried to get together as often as possible to take in the sights, see movies, play basketball, shop, or just have a good time. On one such occasion, we gathered in Yanawaa, where Elder Montgomery was living and working with Elders McCormick, Lange, and Griffiths. A more lively district I can hardly imagine. Towel fights were legendary, with Elders McCormick and Lange raising welts on each other the size of golf balls. Elder Montgomery was always an independent sort and Elder Griffiths, while quiet, was deceptively wily.

The Yanawaa house was a large three-story structure with a deck on the top of the third floor. As was typically the case, the front room downstairs was used for meetings, while the second floor was used as living quarters for the missionaries. The third floor was vacant and was used only for towel fights and subsequent triage. Ten of us squeezed into living space for four on one Sunday evening, and after hearing the tale of a very recent robbery at the Yanawaa house where the maid had been stabbed, we ate and then fell asleep-except for Elders Lange and Griffiths, that is.

Elders Lange and Griffiths fidgeted in their beds like two children waiting for Santa Claus to come on Christmas Eve. Their caper had been planned for 3:00 a.m. and was designed to mimic the common place burglaries that missionaries often endured in Thailand.

As if timing were significant to the event, Elder Lange refrained from commencing the affair until precisely 3:00 a.m. On cue, and from his bed, he pulled a strategically placed rope that snaked its way up to the third floor through an outside window. There, his tug pulled a door closed that in turn knocked several blocks and an iron down the flight of stairs from the third floor to the second. The clatter was enough to wake the innocent victims of the prank. Missionaries, like frightened rabbits, sat erect in their beds, listening for sounds and eyeing each other to see if they had been the only ones who had heard the evidence of an intrusion. Elder Griffiths then pulled his rope, which caused an ironing board to fall over on the first floor. With that second diversion having been played out, eight missionaries went scurrying throughout the house, trying to catch a thief.

The other two, Elders Lange and Griffiths, looked on in quiet amusement. I am not sure how their amusement could have been so quiet as I think back at eight missionaries running around the house in their temple underwear. After a time, we all found ourselves on the stairway up to the third floor. The final rope was pulled and the third floor door slammed shut. Eight brave missionaries became utter cowards upon arriving in the hallway, just across from the door that had so recently been slammed shut. All the ropes had been rigged so that, once used, they would come loose and be reeled in, so as to not be discovered by the victims of the hoax.

Nobody wanted to be first inside that third-floor door. After a time, there were several who volunteered to turn the doorknob, but still no takers to actually lead the charge into the room where the most recent noise had been heard.

What seemed like an eternity must have only been about thirty seconds, but no matter. I could not stand the suspense any longer and, standing safely at the rear of the crowd of suspense-plagued elders, I reached through several bodies, turned the doorknob, and pushed-not the door, but the elders. All eight of us went tumbling into the crime scene at once. We were immediately confronted by two wire-framed mannequins dressed up as missionaries. Each was wearing his own distinctive pocket-protector-style Thai nametag, one phonetically sounding out the word *stupid* and the other sounding out the word *dufie*.

We were all so close to hyperventilation at this point that we didn't get the joke. Instead, we looked at each other as if to ask why burglars would set up such strange mannequins. We then continued in our frantic search for the bad guy(s). By now, Elders Lange and Griffiths could no longer sit quietly by. They were ready to accept our congratulations for a prank well-conceived and executed, but we were too entranced by the chase and the potential for danger to realize that it was all a ruse. As we would rush by them, Elders Lange and Griffiths would taunt us with hints. The hints meant nothing to us. We were engaged in a dangerous manhunt.

Only when one of the elders finally discovered a tape recorder strapped to the outside deck of the roof of the third floor, did it dawn on us that we had been had. We rewound the tape that had been running throughout the chase, and listened to the entire proceeding, including the explanation of what was to happen and the sound evidence of what did happen. There was no burglar. The ruse was complete.

Elders Lange and Griffiths would someday have to pay. After all, such a prank could not be left without a response. Boys will be boys, and missionaries are sometimes nothing more than big boys.

The missionary life had become quite comfortable in Nonthaburi. Being a district leader now, I had a few extra paperwork responsibilities, but I had gotten used to the administrative gobbledy-gook of weekly reports and running church meetings. We were experiencing some success reflected by real baptisms, and our attendance at church by investigators was oftentimes reaching up to twenty people. Life was good, and that always meant that moves were on the horizon.

As soon as things settled into a nice, easy routine, I always seemed to be moved to a new location and a new job. This next assignment seemed somewhat ironic in that I was now to work with Elder Mongkon, my Thai-language teacher in Hawaii, and now a gung-ho, diehard, and dead-serious missionary. We were to be the zone leaders in the Central Zone, which meant that much of our job was to be administrators in working with other missionaries. At this point in time, I would have much preferred remaining a proselyting missionary. I had finally become good at something, and now I was not going to be able to do it. Besides, my lighthearted approach to life was viewed by Elder Mongkon as downright destructively light-minded.

In reviewing the move list further, I noticed that Elder Probert was being made a senior companion, and I was somehow pleased, as if I had something to do with it. Vanity, I suppose. As missionaries, we are often asked to do things that are somewhat overwhelming, and I realized that Elder Warner must have felt the same sense of accomplishment when I became a senior companion.

I had one week to make sure that Elder Probert remembered where all of our investigators lived, what discussions they had been given, and what areas they needed to work on. We also reviewed their personal likes, dislikes, their family situations, and any other matters that would help Elder Probert to stay close to our contacts and my friends.

As I conducted my last church service in Nonthaburi, one of my most satisfying moments occurred: Brother Sutchii and his wife and four children all ambled into church, joining us for the first time. It was a good day, and I quietly wept.

XXVI

REMEMBRANCE

The idea of working with Elder Mongkon as a zone leader was not all that pleasant. He didn't particularly like me at the LTM, and I was sure that sentiment had not changed. It is difficult to live with someone who has no real use for you. A missionary simply does not have a whole lot to say about who he works with or where he serves. I suppose Elder Mongkon considered this new assignment to be more of a test than I did, and I considered it to be a bigger challenge than I wanted. In making the move I took solace in a verse from Shakespeare's *As You Like It:*

... Tongues in trees,
Books in the running brooks,
Sermons in stones,
and Good in everything.

I could definitely say that Elder Mongkon spoke Thai better than any of my previous companions. He certainly had the edge on me there, and I correctly figured that I would learn more Thai from him. I was right. I also quickly learned that in dealing with Elder Mongkon, I could do just about whatever I wanted, so long as he thought it was his idea. With that little bit of knowledge in hand, Elder Mongkon and I were actually able to produce two pretty solid months of effort.

As zone leaders in the Central Zone of the Thailand Bangkok Mission, it was our job to make regular visits to the various districts in the zone and work with the missionaries there. Initially, I considered this to be just administrative nonsense that kept me from doing what I had gotten used to...that is, being a missionary. However, my irritation regarding this issue was quickly dispelled on our first visit to Yanawaa and Samut Prakaan *(Sah-MOOT BRAH-gahn)*.

It turned out that while being a zone leader was not that big a deal; it was a position of authority which afforded me a degree of respect that was largely unearned and virtually unchallenged. With that kind of position, it is not hard to see why some can become overbearing, obnoxious, and irritating.

The most difficult part of trying to function as a regular missionary in this new position was our living situation. As in Samsen, our dwelling did not double as a meetinghouse, and we therefore lived in an apartment. But living in an apartment in the central part of Bangkok meant that we were the halfway house for all the missionaries who had to come to Bangkok to renew their visas, see the president, or effect changes in their work assignments. As a consequence, we were not really an apartment of missionaries trying to do a job, but instead we served as the "Hotel *Ekamai*" *(EGG-ah-mai)*. Our roommates were Elders O'Brien (the mission secretary) and Brown (the mission's visa secretary and infamous lizard eater).

On one of our zone leader visits, I had a chance to work with Elder David Lange. Elder Lange and I were from the same congregation in South Pasadena, California, and had entered the mission field just three months apart. We were friends before the mission experience, and so we knew each other as we really were, not just as pious and pure vessels of the Lord Jesus Christ in white shirts and ties. After tracting for the better part of two hours one fine morning, we sat on a large log in the middle of an open rice field to take a break. For a brief time, nothing was said as our eyes took in the vision of the expanse of rice fields and elevated wooden, thatched roof houses all around us, and our minds raced halfway around the world to another time and another place. Finally, after what seemed like the passing of a brief eternity, we just looked at each other and began to laugh uncontrollably. How is it that the two of us, neither of whom were model citizens back home, could have been placed together to do this work on the outskirts of Yanawaa, Thailand? It was more than we could comprehend. It was all quite surreal. We sat on that log a long time, talking about Thailand and our experience there, and then reminiscing about the old days.

There is a certain decorum that is to be maintained as a missionary in the Church of Jesus Christ of Latter-day Saints. Our musing carried us back to a time when we were not as concerned with how we were perceived and how we could maintain a clean image. Some years before our missionary duties made us act much older than we were, David and I had taken a trip to the Colorado River for a week of rafting with my brother Eric and a friend, Kent Wilson. As we were sitting on that log in Yanawaa, Thailand, Eric was serving as a missionary on some Indian reservation in the Dakotas, and Kent was laboring in Guatemala City, Guatemala. We thought about what they were doing, and laughed that it was surely different from the wonderfully carefree days of rafting.

In that time, we had created our own raft to carry us down a quiet part of the Colorado River near Blythe, California. The raft wasn't pretty, but it was functional…sort of. It consisted of six truck inner tubes lashed together, which formed the base of the raft, over which bamboo poles were lashed together to give the raft some structure. Over all of that, we laid a canvas tarp down to provide some semblance of a flat surface. In tow behind our pleasure craft was a smaller flotation device, created out of four automobile inner tubes and a three-foot-by-three-foot piece of plywood that was tied down on top of those inner tubes. All our supplies were carried on this smaller raft that was towed behind us…at least it was behind us most of the time when the raft was pointed straight ahead.

Sitting on the other side of the world, Elder Lange and I relived the lightning storms and the bridge that we did not negotiate carefully enough. We missed the under-crossing space made for boats and instead barely squeezed the raft through the support structure, which provided us with no more than two inches of clearance on each side of the raft. I am not sure I had ever been closer to disaster than when we passed under that bridge on the Colorado River. The raft was barely seaworthy and clearly not something that was easily directed, but it was ours and we did survive.

We remembered that about three days into the rafting trip, we were floating in a leisurely fashion down the middle of the Colorado River. The air temperature had to be better than 110 degrees and the water temperature was comfortably warm. The four of us were lounging on the raft and just enjoying the time to relax, when David announced that we had to go ashore so that he could relieve himself. The rest of us did not have that problem and did not share in his desire to undertake the laborious job of maneuvering our vessel to shore. In unison, we all told David to "pee in the river."

He apologetically responded by explaining, "If that's all I had to do, that would not be a problem."

Kent, Eric, and I eyed each other for about one second following this revelation from David, and then lay back down on the raft, not having been convinced that sufficient cause had been given to undertake any real manual labor. David then reluctantly boarded his rubber raft and allowed himself to drift some forty feet or so from the main raft. He was connected to our raft by a long length of rope.

Some time passed by when we began hearing frantic screams from David. Those screams caused us to look up and see him thrashing about in the water as if he was being attacked. Our immediate concern was that maybe, in fact, he was indeed being attacked by a water snake or some other horrible creature. We immediately began pulling the tether line toward us, drawing David and his small raft closer and closer. After heroic efforts to pull him in, David was close enough for his voice to be understood: "It floats! It floats!"

When it finally became clear as to what he was referring to that floated, we all sat back down onto the raft and had ourselves a great laugh.

Elder Lange and I smiled at the thought of those days that seemed so far away. It was as if they had occurred to someone else in a different lifetime.

XXVII

CHANGING OF THE GUARD

By nature, I am a very relaxed soul; by contrast, Elder Mongkon was not. The first three or four weeks we were together, I heard from his mouth the words *rew rew khaw* at least a hundred times. *Rew rew khaw* means to *hurry up*. His instruction to me was so constantly irritating that I wanted to pop the little guy. But the thought that there was "good in everything" would always come back into my mind, and I realized that I could put up with Elder Mongkon for as long as President Morris wanted to leave us together. After all, Elder Mongkon was putting up with me too, probably a much bigger challenge.

Elder Mongkon's approach to the missionary effort was far different than mine. He was consumed by the thought that so few of his people understood the value of Christianity as taught by the Mormons, and he had a sense that it was his responsibility to his people to share the word with all of them *right now*. While I respected him for that, I wished he could try to share his obsessive zeal with someone else.

Fortunately, Elder Mongkon and I were always surrounded by a whole gaggle of other missionaries. After all, our primary duty was to work with the missionaries in our zone. For the most part, our task was extremely enjoyable. On one day I would meet Elder Humpheries' contacts in Chachernsao (*Chah-CHERN-sauw*), renewing my friendship with him in the process. Then I would go out tracting with Elder Jensen in the afternoon. Elder Jensen was a new missionary from El Paso, Texas, and he could fill me in on all the latest popular music from the States.

The next day, Elder Mongkon and I would be in Chonburi visiting with Elder Daniels and Elder Mantilla. These elders were phenomenally efficient, and on the days we visited with them, we would have eight to ten contact meetings to handle. These two missionaries were almost frightening in their enthusiastic pursuit of their jobs. Each time we visited with them, I remember walking up to their home early in the morning and being greeted at the front door by both of them wearing their missionary white shirts and powder-blue Chinese pajama bottoms. After inviting us in and feeding us breakfast, they would be dressed and ready to go within minutes, and they always had our days fully packed. I would get tired just thinking about all that they were doing, but it was also quite inspirational there.

Another plus was that Chachernsao and Chonburi were beautiful and unspoiled coastal communities. We were told to look for a location for an upcoming zone conference. We had heard of an ideal location some twenty kilometers south of Chachernsao. Since it was our job to set up the zone conference, and since Elder Mongkon would rather be an example of a hard-working missionary than see the sights of his own country, I volunteered to head south and check the facilities out. Sure enough, there was a beautiful hotel and an even more beautiful beach that seemed just right for my kind of zone conference…a little beach volleyball, some football, and nice meeting rooms for some semblance of an actual training session. Elder Mantilla and I boned up on all the particulars, and I returned to Bangkok chock full of information for the zone conference.

The newly arrived Elder Jensen represented what seemed to be a different breed of missionary from what I was used to. These new elders had not shared any of the experiences I had been living through over the past year-and-a-half, and I had been completely removed from any of the experiences they had been undergoing prior to their coming to Thailand. While I enjoyed the younger elders, I certainly did not feel a part of them. The feeling was noticeably mutual as they looked at me as some kind of old dog just coming back from war. The difference in terms of experience was marked. I began to realize that I had effectively buried the Ross Palfreyman that was and, at least for the sake of this mission, replaced him with the Elder Palfreyman who was to proudly and boldly serving in God's Mormon Army. I supposed that these younger missionaries would in time take my place as the old dogs and then feel the same sense of separation from the younger elders that I was now feeling.

Upon sharing the information I had gathered for the upcoming zone conference with Elder Welling, who was now an assistant to the President, I was quietly advised that I would not be enjoying the zone conference anyway, as I was about to be moved to Udorn *(OO-dorn)* in the northeast of Thailand. I was not as pleased as I thought I would be when I heard the news that I would no longer be working with Elder Mongkon. We had actually worked out a sense of space between us and were able to stay off of each other's toes. He had actually stopped hounding me to "rew rew khaw," and my habit of flipping bottlecaps everywhere we went had become a pleasure that I participated in only in Elder Mongkon's absence.

Again, I was going to miss the missionaries whom I had been working with, and more than that, I was going to miss the members of the church whom I had come to know. Finally, I also knew that I was going to miss the ease with which you could meet people in Bangkok. There were millions of them. With this new assignment to Udorn, I was now headed back to a more rural environment like Lumphoon, where there would just not be as many people to choose from.

One good thing about the move was that I would no longer be in the heart of the mission's gossip central. Elder troubles, discipline, failures, rumors about missionaries leaving the mission field early, why they had to leave, and so forth, were common topics of conversation in Bangkok.

At least in Udorn, I did not have to hear so much about the unseemly side of the missionary work. I acknowledged the need to be informed of what went on, but sometimes I would just as soon not know. Former Chief Justice Earl Warren's response to a critical comment about his habit of reading the sports page before looking at the headlines of a newspaper was something to the effect that the sports pages happened to be filled with man's successes, while the front page was littered with his failures. I envisioned Udorn as a place to really be able to focus my attention on doing good works for the last three months of my time in Thailand and as a place where I did not have to hear about our failures.

XXVIII

UDORN

Climbing onto my Pat tour bus that would take me to Udorn was a pleasant surprise. I looked into the bus seeing that there were individual seats for each passenger, and that each of the seats actually reclined a little bit, almost like an airline seat. What a deal! I had imagined I would be traveling to Udorn on a regular city-style bus with bench seats and no available seating room for missionaries.

Standing in the back of such a bus for eight hours was not something I had looked forward to. This, on the other hand, was all right.

Elder Richardson and I took our seats next to each other about halfway back in the bus and began chit-chatting about who we were. We had never met prior to being assigned to work together in Udorn as zone leaders, but I had heard Elder Richardson had a difficult time with Elder Warner, who managed to wreck Elder Richardson's self-confidence, even though he was probably the best missionary in the country at the time in terms of his language skills. He was a native of Salt Lake City, had no apparent girlfriends at home, and had a love of chess, which compelled him to carry his chess set on all his journeys. In fact, the first time I ever played Elder Richardson a game of chess was on our Pat tour bus as we both headed to Udorn.

I found out just how low Elder Richardson's self-esteem was the first time we went out to teach. We had met a man in Udorn at a brief street meeting and agreed to teach him in his home the following day, which we did. While Elder Richardson was telling Praphan *(Brah pAHN)* about the Book of Mormon, he became very hesitant when setting forth the details, such as the time frame for the book. He told Praphan that the book covered a span of time from approximately 600 B.C. to 400 A.D. He then turned to me and asked, "Is that right, Elder Palfreyman?"

I nodded and Elder Richardson went on. Several more times during this discussion, Elder Richardson would turn to me and ask if he had correctly stated the facts. While walking home from that meeting, I asked Elder Richardson what was going on that he would ask me for verification of all these nit-picking little facts, which I found to be rather unimportant in the whole scheme of things. Besides, I was not too good at remembering specific details anyway.

He then explained that his prior companion, Elder Warner; "would stop me constantly during our lessons and correct me not only as to facts and details but also as to Thai vocabulary, sounds, and tones that I might be misstating."

He was a missionary who had been absolutely badgered by his prior companion into a state of total lack of self-assurance. I wanted to smack that prior companion, but my feelings only mirrored the feelings of many other missionaries who had crossed his path. I assured Elder Richardson that he would not have that problem with me. I did not have as big a vocabulary as he did for one thing, and for another I did not believe it was worth interrupting a lesson to nit-pick over details. Besides, more often than not, while my companion taught a lesson, I was able to daydream about the sights and the sounds around me. I did not offer that specific information to Elder Richardson, though.

It was quite a new experience for me to sit comfortably on a bus for eight hours without worrying about disturbing any chickens or pigs or other soon-to-be entrée items at someone's dinner table (maybe mine). As I recall, Elder Richardson took the first three chess games on that trip before I knew what hit me. I could only remember back to the days when my little brother, Joel, used to beat the pants off me in chess during our family vacations in Laguna Beach. I was determined to do better in future games.

We took a taxi from the bus station to our new digs in Udorn. As we pulled up to the house at about six o'clock in the evening, we noted that it was quite typical of the other missionary environs I had lived in…with a couple of rather conspicuous exceptions. First, and most glaring, was that it was situated right next door to the local house of prostitution. Being early evening, I spied several of the community's most nubile and available escorts. I was quick to make a mental note that, based upon my own very clear inability to keep my eyes off of these local goods, it was probably not an ideal location for a church.

The second unique observable characteristic of this particular house was that the landlord had placed plywood over at least one window in every room in the house. It was a phenomenon that on my own I could not understand. Our very friendly neighbors quickly clued me in to the fact that we were living in a house that had previously been occupied by the local CIA agents, and that when they had moved on, they had taken all their window air conditioners with them. Boarding over the open window spaces with plywood was a much cheaper alternative than replacing the windows that had been removed to make room for the air conditioning units.

Inside, I met Elder Olson and Elder Atkinson. They rounded out our foursome in Udorn. Elder Olson was my second Canadian missionary encounter, and Elder Atkinson was my second Southern California acquaintance. The former seemed to be having the time of his life in Thailand, while the latter seemed intent on honorably finishing up his missionary duties so that he could get back to the rest of his life as a CPA. Both were exceptional missionaries.

Almost the first night in Udorn, I learned how to make up for the emotional trauma of constantly losing in chess to Elder Richardson. He enjoyed wrestling and since I could pin his ears back nine out of ten times, I too learned that the sport could be quite fulfilling. My prior wrestling experiences with Elder Judkins were not so wonderful. He was just too strong. I remember one time being thrown down on a bed by Elder Judkins so hard that the whole bed frame just collapsed around me. Elder Richardson was just not that physically imposing.

Elder Olson greeted us with congratulations at having been assigned to the best place in Thailand to do missionary work. Initially, I thought that Elder Olson had been listening to too many positive mental attitude tapes, but I was quick to learn that he was absolutely right…Udorn was a great place to be a missionary.

Politically, the United States was abandoning its decade-long struggle to prop up South Vietnam, and as a result, that country, along with Cambodia and Laos, were quickly falling into the hands of communist regimes. The Killing Fields was just beginning and refugees began flowing across the borders into our missionary zone, almost as if they had formed a river. There were stories of terror and butchery that made the entire region rethink its political and social allegiances. The great United States had lost a war and, in the minds of many Thais, had abandoned its loyal ally, Thailand. Communist insurgents were making periodic incursions into the northeast of Thailand, and the Thai people there wanted to know what was to become of them. It seems that whenever there is such social upheaval, people do tend to return to their spiritual roots to seek answers and comfort.

Bunthom *(BOON-toam)* was just such an individual. The elders had met Bunthom one week prior to my arrival in Udorn. Elder Richardson and I taught Bunthom for the first time the afternoon of our first day in Udorn. Bunthom was a very shy young man about eighteen-years-old who had a job working as a ticket taker at the local movie theater. It took Elder Richardson and me about ten minutes of our first meeting with him to know that he truly was interested in learning about the gospel of Jesus Christ. It was also noted that his interest in Western culture and tall, skinny, white people was also a motivating factor for him to spend time with us.

Elder Richardson and I had inherited from our predecessors a travel and conference schedule that required us to leave Udorn only two days after we arrived. Our itinerary took us through Nakhon Phanom *(NAK horn PAH-noam)* and then on to Ubon *(OO-boan)*, after which we would make stops in Mahasarakham *(Mah-HAH-sah-rah-kahm)*, Khon Kaen, and Khorat *(Ko-RAHT)*.

After a one-hour layover in Nakhon Phanom, we took off for Ubon. As we took off in the propeller-driven aircraft that held approximately twenty passengers, I could hear all kinds of little unsettling noises. The pilot's voice was not overly reassuring when he announced that our takeoff required us to pass into Cambodian airspace. "The small arms fire that you hear will not delay or impact our flight in any significant way," we were told over the intercom.

I am sure that my initial facial response to what I had just heard was similar to that of Elder Richardson's. We looked at each other for a moment and then began to laugh. There was not much we could do about it anyway. Elder Richardson pulled out his chess board, and since he was four games up in our ongoing series, I was allowed to move first.

Ubon was a military town...a United States military town, that is. The Americans, as a part of their overall withdrawal from the war in South Vietnam, had closed up shop in Ubon, moving all of its B-52s to other bases. The economic impact was stark and ugly. The tin-roofed and tin-sided shanties that had been constructed stood mostly abandoned and eerily quiet. All that seemed to be left were some unemployed base workers and homeless former live-in prostitutes. I was grateful that I never was assigned to work in such a place. An economic recovery would take some time.

After visiting Ubon, the villages of Mahasarakham, Khan Kaen, and Khorat seemed like little pieces of heaven. I got to say good-bye to Elder Montgomery in Khorat, as he was just moving from that city to Bangkok, where he was to take my place as the zone leader. He asked me if I had made any plans for the return trip home to the States in three months. I had not and was not all that anxious to think about it. The return home was quite frightening to me. It meant going back to a place that I did not fully comprehend. What I did know was that I was expected to return home as an adult and that the child in me was to be vanquished. Going home had become more frightening than any thoughts I had conjured about going out on a mission. I simply did not want to talk about it with anyone.

XXIX

BUNTHOM

Back home in Udorn, Elder Richardson and I met with a Bob Markel. He had a son in Pasadena, California, which seemed to create some sense of connection between us, and he invited us to his home to present our story to him. He was something of a gruff American expatriate who, as best as I could tell, was making his living as an arms dealer. I never had the nerve to ask him which side he was selling to or how one would even get started in such a business. Instead, we mostly talked religion.

Elder Richardson told him the Joseph Smith story of the Prophet's First Vision of God the Father and His Son, Jesus Christ. As Elder Richardson tried to paint a verbal picture of the quiet and peaceful setting in the woods in upstate New York where this vision took place, he was interrupted by Bob, who asked, "It's all too perfect to be true. Why couldn't Joseph Smith simply have been sitting on the john at the time of the First Vision? Why did it have to be out in the serene and peaceful woods?"

Elder Richardson was stumped. Frankly, so was I, but after a moment's hesitation I did respond, saying, "I imagine in those days Joseph Smith would probably have been sitting on the john in a little outhouse behind his residence, and that just maybe God the Father and His Son, the Lord Jesus Christ, and Joseph Smith could not all fit in the outhouse together."

Bob laughed and told Elder Richardson to proceed, as that was as good an explanation as he could imagine. Elder Richardson and I had several additional meetings with Bob Markel, but all the while, we knew it was quite unlikely we would get anywhere with him. Still, we enjoyed his company, and he enjoyed ours. We were about the same age as his son in the United States, whom he had not seen in several years. We seemed quite comfortable using each other to fill certain voids in our lives. We were Bob's surrogate sons, and he was our connection to our past lives in America.

While Bob was a diversion, Bunthom was why we were in Thailand. Elder Richardson and I began teaching Bunthom on a two-times per-week basis. He seemed to be soaking it all in, and more and more I became convinced that he was sincerely interested in the religion we were teaching him and not just looking for a way to hang out with some American "friends."

Elder Richardson and I talked about Bunthom quite often and finally, after praying together about what to do, decided that we would challenge him to be baptized into the church.

In our next meeting with Bunthom, we taught him about baptism by immersion for the remission of his sins. He responded, "I understand that the death and resurrection of Jesus Christ was the Savior's way of saving us from our own sins, and that all I must do to accept the full impact of that gift is to take upon me the name of

Jesus Christ through baptism, and then do my best to live my life in accordance with His will."

Elder Richardson and I were absolutely stunned. We were sure we had never said things that clearly to him in the past and were even more sure that we were not that good at teaching. Regardless, we were elated and set a tentative baptismal date of April 26, 1975. With such a date in place and knowing that Elder Richardson and I traveled frequently to other cities in the northeast of Thailand, we began a more intensive teaching schedule of three times per week. Hopefully, we could get Brother Bunthom ready for baptism at the same time that Elder Olson and Elder Atkinson had scheduled for four of their contacts to be baptized.

Brother Prasert *(Brah-SERT)* had a wife and three children, and had been taking lessons from the missionaries for probably as long as I had been a missionary. He had finally committed to be baptized, along with his wife and two of his three children who had reached the age of eight. His third child, a seven-year-old, would have to wait a year. It was explained to him that the Mormon Church teaches that baptism is reserved for those who can understand what commitments they are making, and little children under the age of eight are presumed not to understand the commitments to be made at baptism. Prior to that time, they are simply saved by the grace of the Lord Jesus Christ's infinite Atonement.

XXX

A SCARE AT THE BORDER

As my visa had again expired, it was time for my last trip to Cambodia, along with my nine remaining compatriots. It was a little sad thinking about going home and contemplating the possibility that I would never see these, my friends, again. But the sad nostalgia of the thought quickly disappeared as we approached Poipet *(POY-pet)*. Cambodia was no longer a pleasant place to be, and the border town of Poipet was no longer considered to be a very peaceful and quiet place. We crossed the border and shopped for temple rubbings, cheap platters, and other knickknacks while our visas were being processed.

At the conclusion of our excursion to Poipet and while we were walking together down the street and back towards the border between Cambodia and Thailand, a Cambodian military helicopter descended from amidst the white billowy clouds and landed between us and the border. Immediately out from the helicopter jumped several military types fully decked out in their battlefield regalia, weapons drawn. Were they after us? Were we five minutes too late in getting back across the border? None of us knew. I eyed the side streets for possible avenues of escape should it come to that. It did not, fortunately, and after a few moments of intense silent prayer on my part, the Cambodian soldiers went in search of other prey. Needless to say, we finished our trek to the Thai side of the border as quickly as possible.

It was interesting that my fear of being captured by the soldiers was more intense than any feelings I had about being killed. It's just that when you are dead, you go home to God. During my two-year stint in the mission field, I never had any fear about reporting in to God and making an accounting for my actions. But being taken captive, well, that was quite another issue. I had a fairly clear perception that being somebody's captive was not a very good idea. It was a relief to know that I would probably never have to do another visa run.

Shortly after I returned to Udorn from Cambodia, the president's assistants, Elders Castleton and Welling, appeared for the purpose of interviewing our five prospective new members. Brother Prasert and his family all were approved for baptism, while Brother Bunthom was asked to wait a month. Brother Bunthom quietly accepted the brief delay, and we began preparing for our first baptisms in Udorn in a long time.

XXXI

WATER FESTIVAL

This year, I was not about to miss out on the fun associated with the Water Festival. Last year at this time, I was in Lumphoon and made several attempts to continue working as if the Water Festival was not a major holiday in Thailand. This year, I was going to enjoy the cultural aspects of the country I was a guest in. After renting a pickup truck and placing two fifty-five-gallon barrels in the back, I filled each with water and then directed my rented truck driver to proceed to various members' homes, where Elders Olson, Atkinson, and I invited them to join us as we rode around town spreading good cheer to all who would be doused by us. (Poor Elder Richardson was sick and had to stay home in bed. He was so sick, in fact, that we later had to take him to the Air Force base in Udorn to be examined and treated by a doctor. Even though the rules absolutely require companions to never separate, I did not have too much concern about leaving him at home alone for an hour or so. He was so sick that he couldn't have done anything wrong even if he wanted to.)

By the time we had rounded up everyone we could think of, we had at least a dozen people loaded into that pickup truck, each with his or her own little bucket. Downtown Udorn was a wonderful place for us to spread our holiday cheer by throwing water on all the merchants and shoppers as they shuffled along the sidewalks in front of the main shopping district. We had to refill the fifty-five-gallon barrels three times before we were all satisfied that we had sufficiently celebrated the Water Festival. I don't remember having a more enjoyable time celebrating a holiday that I didn't quite understand. And as for the relationships among the members, the investigators, and the elders, I don't know that we had ever had a better bonding experience outside of our limited contact with each other through the church.

Elder Richardson continued to be sick for a couple of days, and I would have felt worse for him except that it was a chance for us to play several games of chess during a period of time when he was not able to focus very clearly on his game plan. During his bout of illness, I was able to square up the score at thirty-two games apiece. I knew that when he got better, he would make me pay dearly for catching up with him, but I savored the moment.

We were scheduled to go to Khon Kaen for a long one-day trip when Elder Richardson got better, and that meant we would play two or three games of chess in route. I was anticipating a sweep by Elder Richardson. If he got too full of himself over it, we would simply have to wrestle. The two of us were rather competitive, and we each had to have something we could hold over the other.

XXXII

CIA AGENT

In Khon Kaen, the elders seemed to be doing fine. As usual, we were able to meet with their best contacts and tract in new territory, at least as far as we were concerned. In Khon Kaen, Elder Pope took me to the poorest neighborhood I have ever been in. There were rows upon rows of tiny little shacks that all seemed to be built out of garbage. Tin walls and roofs constituted luxury dwellings. Many of these people had recently relocated to this area from Ubon and Udorn, and other cities that had recently been abandoned by the American military. Thousands of people were out of work and had nowhere to go except for this godforsaken lean-to shantytown.

Elder Pope and I did not stay long, as the stench of human waste and the weight of human depression bearing down on our shoulders was more than we wanted to deal with. I had never been a big fan of visiting Khon Kaen, and after this trip I realized that this would be one part of Thailand, along with Ubon, that I would not miss. I hoped for a better future for both towns.

I said my good-byes to Elder McCormick and Elder Pope and exited their home. Unfortunately, Elder McCormick and Elder Pope had conspired to give me a good-bye dumping into their disease-infested pond. As their rather heavy push made it inevitable that I would be going into the pond, I tried to leap forward in an effort to jump all the way across the pond. I didn't make it and my left shin crashed against the rock embankment on the far side of the pond. The blood did not begin to really flow right away. It was almost as if my body hadn't quite comprehended what had happened to it immediately, and it took some time for my brain to tell my leg to begin bleeding. When it finally did, though, I had a devil of a time getting it to stop.

The big problem was that we had to catch a bus at the Khon Kaen bus station to get back to Udorn because we had several meetings early the next morning. The last bus out of Khon Kaen was leaving in ten minutes, and so I did not have an opportunity to really take care of my little problem. In trying to press a wet rag against my leg enough so that it would stop bleeding, I discovered that I had actually chipped the shin bone, there being a large divot out of the edge of the bone.

I limped to the bus station and got there only to find that the bus was virtually filled to the brim with people and livestock, and that this was to be one of those memorable tests of endurance that you would just as soon not remember. I stood at the back door of the orange-and-grey bus for some time, trying to figure out how to proceed. My left pant leg was rolled up above my knee, and blood was still flowing down my leg and onto my sock and shoe. As a fairly tall American in Thailand, I always tended to draw people's attention, but today a veritable crowd marshalled itself around me, solely to see what this strange American was up to.

I knew that I needed to get on the bus and I knew that I needed ice, and the only other thing I knew was that I did not have time to do both. During my stay in Thailand, I was accused of being a CIA agent on numerous occasions. I was always very careful to try to separate myself from the American government so that there would be no confusion. However, in this case, I believed that a little "white lie" would be appropriate. I looked at four or five young boys standing immediately in front of me and gushed, "I've been shot! I am an American CIA agent and I have been pursuing communists in the jungle right outside of town here. They have retreated, but one managed to get me in the leg. I need ice and I need it now!"

I never saw little boys scatter so quickly. At first, I thought they were simply afraid. But then as some adults who had heard my story helped me onto the bus and cleared off the entire back seat of the bus for me to prop my leg up on, I realized that these people were feeling quite indebted to me for my service on their behalf. Almost the moment I had taken a seat in the back of the bus, replacing two older betel-nut chewing women and a couple of crates of live chickens, several boys came racing to the back door of the bus with plastic bags full of ice for my leg.

I felt quite guilty about the story I had just told, but thanked them for the ice and packed my shin in it as best as I could. Witnessing my plight, my story, and my circumstance, Elder Richardson could not decide whether to scold me for my fib or laugh at the sight of this lowly wounded missionary-turned-American-war-hero in the twinkling of an eye, or more correctly, in the turning of a tale.

XXXIII

GI'S

Arriving back in Udom, I had a new appreciation for the friendship of the Mormon servicemen still living in Udorn. They dutifully helped get me examined and treated by the Air Force base physicians, and after a while, my leg healed up well enough...though I did bring an unwanted parasite home with me who has kept me company ever since.

The Mormon servicemen in Udorn were more than just convenient sources for medical attention; they were my friends. Steve Asay, Rick Duer, John Allen, and Mike Socrates, among others, were always ready to help whenever a need arose. They were not on Mormon missions, though they truly believed and wanted to participate in the missionary effort. While many G.I.'s gave credence to the term "ugly American" by hiring Thai women to be their housemates for a month or two at a time, these Mormon servicemen helped us fellowship people in the community and introduced Thais to us, providing us with additional people to teach. They would help us send boxes home and, in addition to running their own church services on the base, would help us with our services whenever we asked.

Our Mondays in Udorn were never quite the same as our Mondays in Bangkok. Each Monday morning, instead of trying to find a dozen or so other elders in Bangkok, we would ride out to the military base, where the Mormon servicemen would challenge us to games of paddle ball, racquetball, and tennis. It was great exercise and great fun, but it was also very interesting to hear stories of American pilots who were actually involved in a war in South Vietnam but who were not allowed to unleash the full might of their arsenals on the enemy. So, instead, they would oftentimes finish their assigned task and then buzz the streets of downtown Hanoi as they returned to base, breaking and cracking out windows along the way. It sure seemed like an inefficient way to wage war.

The work in Udorn really began to pick up steam. Brother Prasert and his family had all been approved for baptism, and that event would be taking place shortly. It was only a matter of time for Brother Bunthom to be baptized, and there were at least another half a dozen people moving right along toward becoming members of the church. President Morris saw the excitement in Udorn and sent two more missionaries up to join us: Elders Day and Carlson, both Utah boys. They would both become junior companions in our district, under the care and keeping of Elders Olson and Atkinson. Six missionaries in Udorn. It was like a feast for us. The camaraderie of missionaries significantly impacts how rewarding a mission is, and the addition of two more missionaries in Udorn made life much more enjoyable. Also, these two missionaries got to move in on several baptisms and would be a part of several more. The fun could be measured by Elder Atkinson's enthusiasm. He no longer spoke of the CPA life at home. Udorn was precisely where we all wanted to be.

Sister Deng and Brother Sawan *(Sah-WAHN)* had both recently committed to baptism. Now there were seven who would be joining the church within the next month or two. In addition to that, several more people who were regularly taking the lessons and attending church in our living room on Sunday swelled our Sunday meetings to eighteen to twenty people each week. After almost two years in the country, it was quite rewarding to see some really positive results.

Elder Richardson and I spent some time looking for a baptismal site. After all, up until then, we hadn't needed one. The hotels didn't seem too excited about letting us use their swimming pools. We realized all of a sudden that we were not too sure where we were going to do this. Baptism by immersion became something of a challenge, and the scaled-back Catholic version of sprinkling took on a new, though limited, appeal.

XXXIV

BAPTISM

President Morris called and asked if I had any travel preferences for returning home, as my two-year stint was about over. I couldn't believe my ears. The end was near, and I did not want to go.

Outside, the monsoon rains were pouring down, and I knew that in an hour I would be out on my bike riding through sunshine. The sun's rays would be so bright that they would penetrate my very being. The monsoon rains would have settled into the many canals and rice paddies that surrounded Udorn, and at this time of year the rice crops would be pushing their way up through the water in the paddies, creating a spectacular green covering to the mirror-like reflections coming off of the standing water. An occasional slow-moving water buffalo would be seen on the levies between the rice paddies, carrying its load of small children. Friendly people, living from day to day and in no particular hurry to change the world or accomplish miracles, would greet you at every turn.

I did not want to go home. At home, expectations were different. President Morris exhorted us to find a wife, settle down, and raise a family. It was absolutely frightening. My first thought was to ask... and I did, "Can I stay an extra three months?"

President Morris was firm. "Everyone else in your group is going home on time. I cannot let you travel alone. Elder Welling has to get home before his little brother leaves on his mission to New Zealand. Elder Humphreys has to get home to help bring in the hay."

Similarly, all the rest of the missionaries in my group were going home to resume their normal lives. Several had planned trips to see certain sights along their way, others had decided to just return straight home. All I could say to the president was, "Keep me here as long as you can, and send me home with the last missionary to leave from my group."

What was I supposed to do? I hadn't given this a serious thought in two years. Now, all of a sudden, it was upon me, and I had no idea what was next. I concluded that the best thing to do was to continue not thinking about it and spend the last four weeks in Thailand doing what I had been doing for the past two years. After all, I was sublimely content.

It was easy enough to ignore going home. We had several imminent baptisms in Udorn to prepare for, and Bunthom's was just weeks away. Brother Asay from the military base suggested that we ride out on one of the highways east toward Cambodia. There, he assured us we would find a picturesque spot to perform the service. Elder Richardson and I hopped on our bikes and rode the five miles out to the lotus flower pond that Brother Asay had described to us. Indeed, it was beautiful, sitting in a park-like setting off the side of the highway. Brother Asay agreed to give a talk at the baptism. After announcing to our few members and our investigators the time and place of the baptism, we excitedly awaited the day.

On that wonderfully charged Saturday morning, we arrived at the lotus pond early, a little bit anxious about how many people would actually show up. Would those who had agreed to accept baptism indeed be there? As our meeting commenced, we had more than thirty people with us, including our four newest members-to-be. Elder Richardson interpreted for Brother Asay, who spoke about the love of Jesus Christ and His sacrifice for our sins. Sister Rose then explained the symbolism of baptism by immersion, that being buried in the water was representative of death and that being lifted up out of the water was representative of a new birth, a birth in Jesus Christ. It was truly a beautiful day. Elder Atkinson and Elder Olson took their turns baptizing Brother Prasert and his wife. Two witnesses made sure that their bodies were fully immersed, and Elder Richardson and I watched for snakes.

Then it was Brother Sawan's turn to be baptized. I was asked to perform the baptism. It had taken me almost two years to do what I had come to Thailand to do…baptize somebody. I had taught several people who ultimately became members of the Mormon Church, but I had never actually baptized anyone in the whole two years leading up to this day. It was a moment of ultimate contentment for me, and if Brother Sawan had even a small degree of the feelings I had, it was also a spiritually fulfilling and peaceful day for him.

No snakes, no mishaps, and only good feelings were present that day. Those non-Mormons who witnessed the affair could only have been favorably impressed. Bunthom was simply beside himself, and could not wait until it was his turn to be baptized. For the week or so that passed between this baptism and Bunthom's, we taught him every day except one. On that one day he invited us to the movie theater, where he had been promoted to assistant manager. The movie was a Thai film with a title that had some connection to the thought that love would ultimately win out. In watching it, Elder Richardson and I could only laugh. It was an exact knock-off of *The Graduate* with Dustin Hoffman back home.

As beautiful as the baptisms had been, Elder Richardson and I vowed to each other that we would find an appropriate pool at a hotel so that the next baptism, the baptism of Brother Bunthom, would take place in a more formal setting. Ultimately, we did convince one hotel in Udorn to accommodate our needs and provide us with the use of their swimming pool. We thought we had good news for Bunthom, but we were wrong.

As we informed Bunthom of our plans, he correctly pointed out to us that the baptisms which had just taken place could not have been any more perfect. As if it was really our decision anyway, he then asked if we would allow him to be baptized at the lotus pond. He was right. In our zeal for order, we had forgotten the absolute beauty and wonder of the events of one week prior.

Brother Bunthom was baptized at the lotus pond. This was a young man whom I had taught the gospel of Jesus Christ to from beginning to end. I had influenced, I think for good, his life. Up to that point in time, I had done nothing more meaningful in my life than that. As I lifted his upper body from the pond, I was at peace with myself and with my God. At the conclusion of the baptism, we headed for the market in downtown Udorn for fruit shakes and *Khao Niao Mamuang (kauw nee o mah-MOO-ahng)*. *Khao Niao Mamuang* was in season. It was by far the best dessert in Thailand and arguably the best food created by God on this earth. Freshly sliced Thai mangos over sticky rice, topped with sweet and condensed milk. It just doesn't get better than that, and my thought was, "How can I ever find such a food back home?"

That night, I reluctantly boarded a Pat tour bus with Elder Day, who accompanied me to Khorat, where I was to conduct some training meetings with the missionaries on a new set of missionary rules. It was strangely ironic that the last thing I would be responsible for as a missionary would be to terminate some of the simple pleasures I so much enjoyed as a missionary: reading the Bible, or other good books in English, listening to contemporary music, traveling beyond district boundaries on days off, and so forth. Surely, the missionary efforts of the church in Thailand had now been domesticated. Independent thinking, creativity, and exposure to life were all slowly being fenced by rules and guidelines. I felt sorry for the missionaries remaining who would experience a far more limited adventure. Organization does bring order, but with it comes a stifling of the individual soul.

All of a sudden, I felt very tired having to meet with all the missionaries in Khorat, Khon Kaen, Mahaasarakham, Ubon, and my own district of Udorn. I was spent. I had now imposed a new set of rules that I did not wholeheartedly support. It was just not a good feeling.

I returned to Udorn where Brother Bunthom was waiting to take Elder Richardson and me to another movie. It was very pleasant. As usual, Brother Bunthom was thrilled to provide us with movie tickets, popcorn, and a Coke, and I was more than relieved to retreat back into the sense of freedom I had in just doing my job of being a missionary and spreading the gospel of Jesus Christ to people who had not previously known Him.

Sister Aan *(Ahn)* was making very rapid progress through the discussions. She was also a pleasure to teach, being very bright and attractive to boot. The latter attribute is always important to a twenty-one-year-old boy whether he is a missionary or not. I was able to teach Sister Aan periodically because as a zone leader I rotated going out with each of the missionaries in the zone on a regular basis.

The best such job was when I could stay home in Udorn and work with the missionaries whom I actually lived with. Elder Day and I spent an evening together tracting, attending a street meeting, and teaching Sister Aan. We taught her about baptism and reviewed the recent baptisms she had witnessed. We then challenged her to prepare herself to be baptized. She accepted. It was a very good night.

XXXV

SPIRITUAL HELP

The next morning, I worked with Elder Olson. We decided to hop on our bikes and tract out some new turf. After riding several miles out of town, we came upon a small village and dug up the patriarch (not literally). We counted ourselves successful because, once the patriarch was in hand, he would gather together most of his clan around him, and instead of speaking with one or two people, we would have an audience of twenty to thirty.

The patriarch's house was stately for the area. It was composed of a wood-sided, box-shaped structure with a tin roof. Inside, there was a large front room that completely opened out onto a deck with a small back room that we never saw. Elder Olson and I were invited up the approximately ten-foot ladder to get to Wisit's *(Wee-SEET's)* house on stilts. People gathered around in the house, on the deck, and on the ground below. I marveled at the beautiful view of open fields, rice paddies so green that they looked alive, and the smallish hills beyond.

We were far enough out into the hinterland that while these people spoke Thai, they were much more comfortable speaking the Northeastern dialect. Elder Olson had become rather good at chit-chatting in the Northeastern dialect and could squat on his haunches for hours on end. He seemed right at home as he squatted down and began explaining who Jesus Christ was and why His message could bring peace and joy into these people's lives.

It was not too long, however, before several of the younger adults began making fun of Elder Olson and his message. It was rather unusual for Thais to make fun of anyone's religion. They were virtually always respectful, and therefore such a deviation was somewhat rare, particularly out in the country. The taunting continued on and Elder Olson redoubled his efforts to overcome it, but was unsuccessful. Finally, one of the antagonists asked, in reference to what tangible reward he could expect if he accepted our message, "Will He give us riches?"

With that, I stepped forward from the side of the deck into the middle of the group and I asked the squirrelly little antagonist, "Do you really want an answer to your question?"

I am not sure if it was my towering over him as I asked the question, if it was the force of my voice, or if it was something else well beyond my own presence, but our sniveling little antagonist sheepishly nodded his head as he bowed down, letting his eyes rest upon the slats of the deck below him. Everyone else present quieted down and turned their eyes toward me.

"God will make you great! He will make you rich. If you will accept His word and live according to it, not only will you be saved in the next life, but you will be made rich in this life!"

I went on to compare the riches of America, a Christian country, to the poverty that surrounded them and their circumstances. I proceeded by challenging, "What great riches has Buddha brought to you?"

I then testified to them of the divine nature of the Lord Jesus Christ and of His divine mission. I went further, saying, "God sent Elder Olson and me to this village on this day to give you the word that God lives, that He sent His Son Jesus Christ to earth as a sacrificial lamb for your sins, that through the death and resurrection of Jesus Christ all mankind will be saved from the grave. By accepting Jesus Christ as your Savior and living your lives according to His word, you will live in peace with God forever."

I finally explained to them that all of God's children will get a chance to hear His word, whether it be in this life or the next, and that this was their chance to accept God, and there would be no other. I then handed Wisit a couple of brochures that had our address on them and admonished him to give serious thought to what I had just told him. I concluded by saying that I was leaving the country to go home, but that there would be others at the address on the pamphlet who could answer any questions he might have. I said good-bye and then Elder Olson and I descended the stairs, climbed on our bikes, and rode away across the dirt road which wound through Wisit's many rice paddies.

Once we had ridden out of sight of Wisit's house, I pulled over and climbed off my bike. I felt somewhat confused and very tired. My belief was that all people would have a real and legitimate chance to hear, understand, and embrace the Gospel of Jesus Christ. I had never believed that missionaries with our pathetic language skills and our youthful inexperience would be the only access that the children of God would have to the gospel, but that was exactly what I had told Wisit and his family. I had also told them that they would become materially wealthy by accepting Jesus Christ. What an abhorrent thought, that you would be motivated to follow Jesus Christ because he could make you rich. I never believed that before, and I don't like it now, but I said it just the same.

Elder Olson then pulled out his word card and asked me the meanings of several words that were spoken in our meeting. It was a missionary's way to improve his language skills to write down words that he heard but did not understand, and then later ask what their meanings were, or look up the meanings in the dictionary. To each of the words Elder Olson had written down I had to acknowledge that I did not know what they meant. Each time he responded by saying, "But you said them."

They were words from the Northeastern dialect, and I simply could not explain what they meant or how they came from my mouth. All I knew was that I was tired, and I wanted to go home. I was not sure what to make of it.

As we rode slowly back toward our house in Udorn, I thought about some of the television preachers that I had seen in the United States who babbled a bunch of gibberish and then claimed to have some insight into the meaning of it all. But to me, that does not seem to constitute any useful gift of tongues; instead, it seems outrageously stupid. On this day, I came to understand that the gift of tongues, in a spiritual sense, is an allowance by God for one to speak to another, even though their languages are dissimilar. It is not meant to confound, confuse, or impress. It truly is meant to be a "gift."

XXXVI

HOME

Once back home in Udorn, I began to pack my belongings for the trip that would end my mission. Two years gave me an opportunity to accumulate a lot of junk that for some reason I was not willing to part with. The problem was that I clearly could not carry it all home; they would have had to give me my own plane. The solution to the problem was Steve Asay, Rich Duer, and John Allen, who came by from the base to say their good-byes. When they saw the pile of mostly junk that I had before me, they offered to send it home for me. It was such a small favor, but it almost brought me to tears. These members were always so willing to help; it was as if they were serving their missions right alongside of me. I had met so many wonderful people in Thailand, missionaries who continue to be my best friends fifty years later, American members whose help and assistance along the way, showed me love and caring for something well beyond themselves and most importantly, the Thai people themselves, who taught me by their lives that America and the Mormon Church do not hold the exclusive rights to virtue in this world, something I had assumed based on very limited experience.

I could not help but reflect on Brother Mani's diligence and dedication to Jesus Christ in the face of family scorn and public ridicule and abuse, and the spirit that I could see through Sister Phatcharaphon's eyes as she contemplated and then accepted the precepts Elder Kirby and then Elder Warner and I taught to her. And I will always hold dear to me the blossoming of the church in Udorn, the unity of the faith there, the opportunity to teach and baptize Brother Bunthom, and my last companion, Elder Richardson. Finally, my many experiences had convinced me that God did live and did love me. I could not ask for a finer end.

Now was the time to go home. I had not told my parents when I was going to return home because I did not want to think about it. All I knew was that I was to report to the mission home on June 6, 1975. When I arrived there, I was greeted by Elder Lange. I could not understand why he was so envious of the fact that I was going home. At that moment, I would have given anything to trade places with him and let him go home so that I could stay.

He asked if I had heard the news of Dara Doney. I told him I had not, and that in fact, I had not heard from her in the past two months. He laughed and said, "She eloped to Las Vegas in February." We had written back and forth over almost the entire course of my two years in Thailand. In the many years since my return from Thailand, she and I have probably only spoken a handful of words to each other. We were best friends up until that time. I have missed her friendship.

President Morris drove me to the airport and thanked me for my service. A better man I have never met. I miss him.

After disembarking the plane at Los Angeles International Airport, I called home and talked to my mother, announcing, "I'm at the airport."

In an almost breathless tone, my mother asked, "Which airport?"

I told her that I was at LAX, and she then asked, "Do you want me to come and pick you up?"

"You don't need to. I am sure there is a bus," I replied.

Looking back on it now, there was something quite eerie about this conversation. Most missionary homecomings include great fanfare and hordes of people waiting at the airport gate for the triumphant return of their missionary hero. Nobody even knew I was home. It was my own fault. I felt lost, alone, and very frightened.

After telling my mother where I would be waiting for them at the airport, I hung up, sat down, and waited. All these years later, the only real emotion or thought that comes to mind about that waiting is fear. I had no clue as to what was ahead. Sometimes in my life, I have not really cared what was ahead. Other times, I have been so absorbed in the present that what was ahead did not matter. But sitting in the airport waiting for my parents to come and pick me up was the first day of the rest of my life. I did not know what I was going to do that evening, the next day, or the next year. Somehow, I had become completely lost.

After a time, I saw the entire family drive up in the green Country Squire station wagon with the fake wood paneling on the side, the same car we had when I left for Thailand. Tommy and Betsy clamored out of the back of the station wagon, while Jeff and Joel jumped out each side of the back seat. Finally, my mother stepped out of the front seat and all were scanning the airport for me.

I panicked. I immediately jumped back behind a broad post and sunk to my knees. It was as if I was reporting to a fate that was not my own. My time in God's Mormon Army had ended. My mission was over.

EPILOGUE

History is a tricky business. Our perception of events and people change over time and, as those perceptions change, so history evolves. A couple of simple examples will illustrate the point here:

Bill Buckner was one of my favorite Los Angeles Dodgers. He moved to the Cubs and then to the Red Sox where, in 1986, he became infamous in game 6 of the World Series against the New York Mets. The Mets were batting in extra innings, and speedy Mookie Wilson hit a slow ground ball towards first base and through Bill Buckner's legs for an error. Ray Knight scored from second base, and the Mets ultimately won game six and went on to win the World Series in seven games. Red Sox fans felt that the "Curse of the Bambino" had struck again, keeping them from a World Series championship, something that had eluded them since Babe Ruth was traded from the Red Sox to the Yankees in 1919. Buckner was blamed for the disappointing loss. He received death threats and was mercilessly heckled for his error, taking all the blame for the loss.

Years went by and the Boston fans softened, realizing that other factors contributed to the Red Sox continued drought relative to the World Series. Buckner returned to Boston some years later and was given a standing ovation, signaling that the historical perspective as to how the World Series was lost had changed, from Buckner's singular error to a series of failures that combined for the actual result. Buckner played in the major leagues for 22 years, batted .289, with 2715 hits, 1208 runs batted in and 174 home runs. Defensively, he made only 128 errors in 13,901 chances. He had a stellar career. From perceived goat, immediately following his infamous error, to a quality player with a solid career. Facts didn't change, but the perspective did. Historical facts didn't change, but time allowed for reflection.

Vietnam war veterans came home from the war to jeers, disrespect, and derision. Americans were being lied to by the government and government policy was without clear direction. Atrocities were being leaked out and soldiers were blamed for all the confusion and ugliness. It took years for American Vietnam veterans to gain a measure of deserved respect.

Again, history didn't change, but perception did. Facts are what they are. But time and experience can change how facts are perceived. I first wrote *Two Years In God's Mormon Army* out of my journal that was written contemporaneously with my time in Thailand (1973 to 1975). My age at the time of the mission was 19 to 21. The first edition of the book, while written from the journal as a primary source, was written over a period of time spanning several years beginning some 15 to 20 years after the actual events and their recordation as a book. Between the actual events and the writing of the book, I finished college at Southern Utah University, graduated from the University of Southern California law school, got married, had a half a dozen kids, and started paying a mortgage. My perspective had changed. Another decade, almost two, has passed, and now, I have added seventeen grandchildren, put in 40 plus years as an attorney, and time has made me see things a little differently once again.

With all three stages of writing, I was as accurate as I possibly could be. But each time, my life experiences impacted how I viewed the same factual events and, therefore, my reporting changed…even if only a little bit each time. More accurate facts came from first-person accounts. My travel through life has made me less judgmental, and that has softened my perspective of all those I have come in contact with, including companions and friends. There are now three versions of the same set of events…the journal, the first edition, and now the second edition. Which is more accurate in reporting what was my *Two Years In God's Mormon Army* was about? I'll take my chances with this second edition, which has the advantage of factual input from other sources, and with the passage of time, has given me perspective based on time to reflect.

GLOSSARY OF "MORMONEZE" TERMS USED IN THIS BOOK

1. Patriarchal blessing - A blessing given to members of the Mormon Church one time in their lives to give them insights as to what their ultimate destiny in life might be and to give them guidance as to how to pursue that destiny. Only a male member called a patriarch, which is an office in the Mormon priesthood, can pronounce these patriarchal blessings.

2. The Brethren (General Authorities, Lord's Anointed) - The Mormon Church is comprised of the President, who is also considered to be a modem-day prophet. The President has two counselors. The President of the church presides over a Quorum of Twelve Apostles. The President also presides over the Presiding Bishop of the church and the Presiding Bishop's two counselors. A step below the Quorum of the Twelve Apostles is a body of leaders called the Quorum of the Seventy. At this point in time, there are five Quorums of the Seventy. It is anticipated that once these Quorums of the Seventy are fully staffed, they will each be comprised of seventy members.

3. Language Training Mission (LTM) - Many of the missionaries sent out each year are assigned to areas of the world that require a working knowledge of a foreign language. By and large, the missionaries are not prepared in the language that is required of them. Consequently, for the first two months of their service, the missionaries participate in an intensive language training course, studying the language of the country they are assigned to. The training facility was called the Language Training Mission. This phase of a missionary's training now usually takes place at the Missionary Training Center (MTC).

4. Endowment - The endowment, in its most simple terms, constitutes a contract between a member of the church and God. Individuals in the Mormon Church commit to obey God's word, sacrifice on His behalf, and obey the laws of chastity and consecration as set forth in the scriptures. In exchange for our promises to conform to these obligations, God promises to not only bless us with eternal life, but also, to grant us "exaltation." Exaltation is the belief that we can live as married couples forever and become like God Himself, ruling worlds of our own. A Mormon tenet is "As man is, God once was; as God is, man may become." In order to pursue this state of exaltation in the eternities, one must conform strictly to the rules of the church.

The endowment (or contract) is entered into in the temple. Once you can honestly assert your worthiness, you are allowed to enter the temple and commit to the contractual terms outlined in the endowment. Worthiness to enter the temple is based largely upon one's abstinence from alcohol, tobacco, tea, coffee, and illegal drugs; fidelity with one's spouse or abstinence from sexual relationships if you are single; a commitment to an unquestioning support of the

General Authorities; and paying a full tithing to the church. Tithing is defined scripturally as one-tenth of one's increase.

Not all Mormons can attend the temple because not all Mormons comply with all these requirements. Hence, those members of the church who do enter the temple and contract with God through the endowment are referred to as endowed members.

If you are not endowed and your marriage is not performed in the temple, then it is believed that your marriage terminates at your death. Only those who have undertaken the endowment and who thereafter seal their marriage in the temple can hope to have a marriage that lasts into the eternities.

5. Brother/Sister - Members of the church commonly refer to each other as brother or sister. Mormons believe in a literal familial relationship between themselves and God the Father. As all are the spiritual children of God the Father, then all are brothers and sisters to each other. Consequently, at church meetings, John Smith is called "Brother Smith."

6. Elder - The term elder can be somewhat confusing. General Authorities are referred to as elders. However, the term elder is also applied to all male Mormon missionaries and is also a reference to a certain office within the priesthood of the church. (See "Melchizedek Priesthood" below.)

7. Investigator - In short, a prospective member who has expressed some interest in the Church. An investigator is one who has been identified as a person to whom attention should be focused on in terms of friendship and Mormon gospel instruction. This person has been targeted for possible conversion to Mormonism.

8. Proselyting - Proselyting is the act of spreading the doctrine and culture of the Mormon Church, with the goal of converting people to the church. It is the main duty of a Mormon missionary (via tracting, conducting street meetings, and other activities) and to all Mormons by extension.

9. Doctrine and Covenants - The Mormon Church believes the Bible to be the word of God. Mormons also believe in continuing revelation from God to the prophets. Based on that belief, the scriptures are not viewed to be closed, but rather living and dynamic. Additional books of scripture in the Mormon Church include the *Book of Mormon,* which is a history of people on the American continent between the years 600 B.C. and 400 A.D., and the *Pearl of Great Price,* a collection of ancient revelations to Moses and Abraham, and more current treatment of doctrinal beliefs in Joseph Smith's time. A fourth book of scripture in the Mormon Church is the *Doctrine and Covenants.* Basically, the *Doctrine and Covenants* is a collection of revelations received by Joseph Smith and succeeding prophets. This collection of scriptures has been accepted by the General Authorities and the church members as scripture with equal standing to the Bible.

10. Word of Wisdom - The Word of Wisdom is contained in Section 89 of the *Doctrine and Covenants* and is founded in a belief that the physical body is the temple of our spirits. As such, the body is to be kept clean and holy. Taking things into the body that degrade or injure it is discouraged. Tobacco, alcohol, tea, and coffee have all been identified as substances not fit for consumption by members of the Mormon Church.

11. Golden contact - In the course of trying to locate individuals or families to teach (read investigators), missionaries will occasionally run across an individual or a family who is so receptive to the word that it becomes pure joy to teach them. These investigators are golden contacts—it is as if you have actually discovered gold.

12. Priesthood (Aaronic and Melchizedek) - The power of the priesthood is the power to act in the name of God. It is the God-given authority to perform various ordinances and to act in certain situations in God's name. (It is comparable to the authority claimed by Catholic priests, bishops, cardinals, and the pope.)

There are two levels of priesthood authority in the Mormon Church. The lower level derives its name from Aaron, the brother of Moses. The Aaronic Priesthood is broken down into three offices: deacon, teacher, and priest. The normal process of progression in the priesthood is for a young male at age twelve to be ordained a deacon in the Aaronic Priesthood. In that position, his most visible duty is to pass the sacrament (similar to the Eucharist) to the members of the church each Sunday. At age fourteen, a young male member is then promoted to the office of teacher. The most visible duty of a teacher is to prepare the sacrament before each Sunday meeting. At age sixteen, a young male Mormon is then set apart as a priest. As a priest, a young man's most visible duty is to bless the sacrament that is then to be passed to the congregation by the deacons. Priests can also baptize new members of the church.

The higher level of priesthood authority in the church is named after the Old Testament prophet Melchizedek. It too, is divided into three offices, the first office being elder. The Melchizedek Priesthood and the office of elder are traditionally conferred upon young male Mormons at the age of eighteen, immediately prior to their leaving on a mission. At about the same time, young Mormon men who are pronounced worthy also proceed to the temple to take out their endowment. (Women, by contrast, do not directly participate in the holding of priesthood offices and wait to enter the temple until they are to be married or until they embark on their own missions at the age of nineteen.) Virtually all male missionaries in the church are elders in the Melchizedek Priesthood. Elders' responsibilities include preaching, teaching, and seeing to the temporal or worldly needs of the members.

The next office of the Melchizedek Priesthood, is that of a seventy. At various times in the church's history, a limited number of Melchizedek Priesthood holders in each congregation were called to the office of seventy. Their job was to seek out and teach investigators.

The third level is the office of the high priest. Basically, the high priest is charged with presiding over the congregation and its members. The high priest, as presiding officer, sees to the temporal and spiritual well-being of the members and the administration of the church. High priests are usually, but not always, the older male members of a congregation, and elders are usually younger.

13. Plan of Salvation - The Plan of Salvation is the Mormon Church's road map defining who we are, where we came from, why we are here, and where we are going.

Before we came to this world, we lived with God. While He had a tangible physical body, we did not; we existed as spiritual off spring of God the Father. In order to become like Him, physical bodies and free agency (or, in other words, a freedom to choose) were necessary.

To facilitate those needs, the earth was created and our spirits have been allowed to enter physical bodies. We do have freedom to make choices in this lifetime, and ultimately, we are responsible for those choices. Sometimes, we make bad decisions, creating consequences that we cannot make amends for, on our own.

Jesus Christ, as God's eldest Son, was designated as our Savior in the premortal existence. He volunteered to come to earth and live a perfect life. He also volunteered to give up His earthly life as a sacrifice for all of our sins. Mormons believe that "no unclean thing can enter into the presence of God" and therefore, if our mistakes are not compensated for, we would be lost. Through Christ's atoning sacrifice, we can have hope of returning to live with our Heavenly Father after our deaths in this life.

It is believed that upon death, our spirits enter into a spiritual world that is divided into two parts. The first is called Paradise and is for those who have successfully navigated their way through life in a manner that is pleasing to God. Spirit Prison, on the other hand, is for those who did not make enough correct choices in their lives, as well as those who were not exposed to the "true" gospel message. It is here that they will be taught, and will have the opportunity to accept it or reject it.

This existence as spiritual beings is temporary. Through the infinite atonement of Jesus Christ, all people will be resurrected, meaning that they will ultimately regain physical bodies as temples for their spirits. It is believed that those physical bodies will be perfected bodies, never again to be worn down by time, disease, or aging. It is also believed that all who come to this world will be provided with resurrected bodies, regardless of whether their acts on earth were good or not. Hence, it is by the grace of God that we all are resurrected, not by any earthly acts of our own.

Upon resurrection, there surely will be a judgment of our acts and deeds in this lifetime. Based upon the choices that we made during our lifetimes, we will find ourselves placed in one of three kingdoms.

They are the Telestial Kingdom, the Terrestial Kingdom, and the Celestial Kingdom. There is also a place called Outer Darkness, that some would say, is the Mormons' equivalent to hell.

It is believed that only a handful of people who lived or will live on this earth will be cast into Outer Darkness. Even most of the dregs of our societies today are believed to be headed not to Outer Darkness, but to the Telestial Kingdom. Joseph Smith once said of the Telestial Kingdom that if we knew how wonderful it was there, many of us would kill ourselves to get there. While it is apparently a nice place, it is believed that God does not dwell there, and that therefore, those finding themselves in the Telestial Kingdom would be cut off from the presence of their spiritual Father.

The Terrestrial world is considered the middle kingdom and is established for those who lived honorable lives, but were "not valiant in the testimony of Jesus" *(Doctrine & Covenants* 76). It is said that while God does not live in the Terrestrial Kingdom, His Son Jesus Christ would visit the middle kingdom.

The Celestial Kingdom is reserved for those children of God who lived lives in accordance with His gospel. They loved Him and made Him a focal point of their lives. Consequently, they also loved their neighbors. For those who attain the Celestial Kingdom, it is believed that they will live with God and His Son Jesus Christ, and that progression for them is eternal, so much so that they may ultimately become like God, in that they can become kings and queens of their own worlds.

Mormons believe that all people will have a full opportunity to participate in this Plan of Salvation. If not afforded the opportunity to embrace the gospel in this life, then an opportunity will be presented in the spirit world. Otherwise, the plan would not be just.

ACKNOWLEDGEMENTS

Many thanks are owed to several people who have encouraged my work from the start. Karla Ginger provided me with an invaluable perspective from someone outside the Mormon Church, so that I would ultimately produce a work understandable to those who know little about the Mormons, their doctrines, or their culture. The glossary at the end of the narrative is a telling example of the results of her input.

Jay Montgomery's encouragement throughout was extremely important. He did not always agree with specific portions of the text, and I dare say that he is not that enamored with all that wound up in print. However, his support of the overall project was unwavering and his acceptance of my need to speak honestly was absolute. To say the least, I am grateful for his support. More than that, though, he is a truly valued friend.

Ken Woolley's opinion has always mattered to me. As usual, it had a positive influence on my treatment of several key topics.

Rosemary Chavez has typed this text through several times for me. She and I have been friends and co-workers for more than a dozen years. Her help in putting the manuscript together has been constant and, at times, heroic.

Tom Palfreyman and Janet Tanner Perry have acted as my editors. Their work clearly showed that I did not pay enough attention to my English course work in college or even high school. Their efforts have made this book much more readable. I appreciate their thoughtful input, which has had a positive impact on the final product. Any remaining grammar issues are mine alone.

Samuel Ross Palfreyman (along with others) and I discussed at length how to organize the text. I thought that using my journal as a guide would make the process simple. It turned out that I had difficulty deciding how to determine chapter content and timing. Should chapters be organized by the cities I was assigned to or by the companions that I had or even strictly by a timeline? Eventually, events determined the creation of chapter divisions. John Ross Palfreyman was a captive son waiting to serve his own mission in Hermosillo, Mexico, in the summer of 2010. He read the book through several times and assisted with many editorial refinements that I had overlooked, despite many prior revisions. For all of that help and his work with the publisher, I am grateful. The book never would have happened without this help. My daughters, Claire Bey, Kate Robinson, Kelly Troutman and Kacey Chaldu, all had to critique the transcript drafts to make sure that I did not step on my tongue at any point. There were a few things that they caught that would have been quite inappropriate.

Gary Shumway took me through the process of actually printing the book the first time. Book Printing Revolution then provided the knowledge and professionalism to provide a marketable product. Paper Raven Books then helped me create a second edition that is more polished and readable. It is nice to be able to rely on those who know what they are doing.

Claralyn has been as steady a friend as I could ever have asked for. Her consistent support through all the drafts, starts, and stops has been invaluable in seeing this project through. Without her steady support this project would never have been completed.

To all, my heartfelt thanks.

www.ingramcontent.com/pod-product-compliance
Lightning Source LLC
Chambersburg PA
CBHW030914120626

46554CB00001B/145